SALATO -
ALL THE BEST ALWAYS

[signature]

NAVY DAYS
MEMOIRS OF A SAILOR IN THE 60'S

E. JON SPEAR

Copyright © 2010 E. Jon Spear
All rights reserved.

ISBN: 1449929583
EAN13: 9781449929589

To my many friends and loved ones, past and present,
Thank you for supporting me so I could be me.

DEDICATION

To the everlasting memory of all of those who served and gave their lives in the performance of their military duties, especially the Pilots and Sailors of the USS Saratoga and the USS Franklin D. Roosevelt, while at sea from 1962 through 1964.

USS Saratoga CVA-60

USS Franklin D. Roosevelt CVA-42

CONTENTS

FOREWORD

By Bert "CatShot" Stevens

Whenever there is trouble in the world that has a potential for threatening the peace of the United States, or our Allies, the first question asked by our leaders is, "Where are the carriers?"

The aircraft carrier is an awesome projection of military power and is capable of delivering the full resources of the United States arsenal. Its mere presence can by itself bring stability to a region.

Carrier operations are dangerous and require people that are well trained and dedicated to the successful completion of the mission. It's a team effort of magnificent proportions. The author of Navy Days was a part of that team for most of his tour of duty.

The flight deck of an aircraft carrier is inherently dangerous during the launch and recovery of aircraft. The average age of flight deck personnel is less than twenty years. Some of them are barely out of high school. Pilots and crewmen put their lives in the hands of these young people and trust them to do their jobs well. They work in a place crowded with aircraft and face the constant danger of being sucked into a jet intake, hit by a prop or blown over the side by a jet blast. The danger they face during day operations is magnified ten fold at night. These young men and women quickly learn the meaning of responsibility and mature beyond their years. We owe them so much.

I was proud to wear the wings of a combat air crewman for four years and to experience flying from a carrier. I came very close to death on several occasions and I am convinced that a higher power intervened on my behalf. I thank all those whose skill and dedication kept me alive.

To all those who lost their lives defending our great country, I say, "God rest your soul and my you know eternal peace."

To those young people that are looking for direction inn their lives, I say "come join our team." You will learn valuable lessons that will be your constant companion for the rest of your life.

To Ed, a friend and the author of "Navy Days," I say thanks for your service and for giving me the opportunity to write a little bit about my own Navy days. Finally, I say to you the words that every sailor wants to hear: "WELL DONE"

PREFACE

Looking back, I would have written about my experiences in the Navy as far back as my post discharge days in 1965. I realized then that my stories were both interesting and entertaining to anyone who expressed an interest as to why I joined, what I did, and what was it like. I told my stories with pride, each time feeling blessed that my early childhood and development enabled me to respond to a calling that would positively influence me the rest of my life. The reason I never wrote it until now is simple. I was too busy getting on with my life and a resume was about the only thing I could write back then.

Navy Days describes my early impressions and development coupled with a desire for change as a teenager in 1960. There was a lot back then; the threat of nuclear war with the Russians, a new president, racial strife, and oh yes, drugs and rock and roll. Being sixteen years old with nothing going on and no future was quite disturbing.

Now, fifty years later, not much has changed with the exception that we are not likely to go to nuclear war with anyone; the war now is against terrorism and drugs. I don't know that the pressures on a sixteen year old today may in fact be worse than they were for me. I find it interesting that President Obama today and President Kennedy in 1960, both emphasized the need and opportunity for "change." Well, the Navy was the opportunity I needed for me to change.

Why did I decide to finally write my Navy memoirs now? I recently saw a movie which was made in 2000, and believe it or not, I had never seen before. It is called, "Thirteen Days," and you can see it on DVD. Basically, it is the story of the buildup and culmination of the Cuban Missile Crisis in late 1962, and how during that short period, we almost went to nuclear war with Russia. What charged me up was seeing my first aircraft carrier assignment, the USS Saratoga CVA-60, in the movie and remembering that I was there at the time.

I hope you enjoy my book whether you are thinking of joining the Navy or are currently serving or are a veteran, like me. I hope you feel enlightened and have fond memories.

ACKNOWLEDGEMENTS

I am deeply grateful to my wife, Megan, my son Eddie and my daughter Lori, for keeping on my back, to write my memoirs about the most critical period in my life. Since my children were kids, they were fascinated by the anchor tattooed on my right forearm, my photos and uniform hanging in my son's closet. Whenever there was a movie about the Navy, I was able to relate my childhood experiences and how I was able to join the Navy to see the world. They loved it, over and over again.

I will never forget my best friends, Cal, Billy, Jimmy, McNeel and Pete, who each in their own way, contributed to me getting on with my life.

Most of all, I will never forget the love and caring bestowed on me by my mom and step-dad, Chas. He knew he was taking a chance letting me join but had the confidence I would turn out okay, which I did. You did the right thing Dad.

Last, as corny as it may sound, thank you President Kennedy. Your words were the inspiration and light at the end of my dark tunnel of complacency and you gave me purpose, something every kid needs.

To everyone, I am forever grateful.

INTRODUCTION

It is 1960, and fear and despair are running deep in America. The United States has many problems at home and abroad. Racial unrest, drugs and a fear of war with the Russians over Berlin, are high on the list. For kids like me, it's all about the beer, the girls and rock and roll. By year end, we elect a new President, John F. Kennedy; the youngest and first Catholic President ever. He touches every young person in America with his promise of change and the protection of freedom.

At that time, my life is going nowhere, and I was tired of being poor and moved around all of the time. Finally, I am forced to move far away from my friends and I find myself at sixteen years old, having to start all over. It is the worst time in my life. I find myself depressed and hanging around with others like me. I didn't really like the feeling and I was getting concerned about my future. My real turning point was when my World History teacher started to talk about our new President elect and the world situation. It captured my interest and listening to him speak made me excited. That coupled with one of my best friends just picking up and joining the marines, planted a seed in my head that started growing as quickly as a 'daffodil' in spring.

At sixteen, I used every possible tactic to get my step-dad to consider letting me do what I now knew was right for me. Fortunately, it worked. I was able to embark on a solo journey, unexpectedly by myself, and join the United States Navy. I actually believe my service changed my life for the better and wonder how I was able to go out on my own.

I truly hope you like my story, and, if there is someone you know who can benefit from an experience like mine, please have them read this book.

My best regards, always, and I hope you enjoy my story.

"Ask not what your Country can do for you;
Ask what you can do for your Country."

President John F. Kennedy
January 20, 1961

ONE
EARLY IMPRESSIONS

It is said much of your character develops during your early years. Fortunately for me, mine started in the 1950's, when life was slow and uncomplicated. There were no distractions compared to today. Electronic games and personal computers weren't invented yet so you had time to observe and learn things. If you were lucky, you had a tiny black and white television in your home. I had a few trucks and a radio and that was fine with me.

I was raised in and around Asbury Park New Jersey, which back then, was the most prominent city on the Jersey shore. About sixty miles south of New York City, it was the summer hot spot with its famous mile long beach and boardwalk, complete with merry-go-round, Ferris wheel and salt water taffy. Even Frank Sinatra knew Asbury Park and referenced it in one of his many hit songs, 'At Long Last Love.'

My mom and I were living in the Fairfax hotel and on nice days she would take me to the beach. She would watch me from the boardwalk while I played in the sand. It was 1948 and I was just about four years old crying about something when she met Charlie, my soon to be step-father. I remember him picking me up and tickling me with his moustache and taking me to the merry-go-round where he worked. Then one day they dressed me up took me with them while they got married. Later when we went back to his house, Charlie had to boost me through a window so I could unlock the front door. He talked me through the whole ordeal and we all laughed when I got it open. It really made me feel good to please them. I never knew I had a real father or that he died when I was two years old. Charlie was the only dad I ever knew.

Charlie worked for an amusement company who oper-
ated the Casino building at one end of the boardwalk. I got
to spend a lot of time there on the merry-go-round and
playing on the beach. Easter Sunday was the busiest time
in Asbury Park. We would get all dressed up and walk the
mile long boardwalk along with another thousand people
dressed up as well. The 4th of July was cool too. When it got
dark, we would watch the spectacular fireworks along the
beach. By the time we got home, I would be sound asleep
and Charlie would carry me into our house.

Right after mom and dad were married, we moved from
the hotel to my dad's house. It was small and out in the sticks
with no other houses nearby. Everything was spread out and
there were few roads and few cars. I really missed the beach
and riding the bus with my mom to the boardwalk. There
were no other houses or kids around so it was just me, my
toys and my yard. One day I found out that we were moving
to a new house. I remember being so exited thinking that
there might be some kids there to play with. As best I could,
I helped Charlie fill the trunk of his big 1937 Buick roadster.
It was black and the most beautiful car I had ever seen. It
even had a spare tire mounted on each fender.

Our new home was in Loch Arbour New Jersey, a small
but very elegant shore community, located just north across
Deal Lake from Asbury Park. Once again we lived back
near the ocean and beaches. Charlie had rented us a garage
apartment behind one of the stately mansions which, along
with the tall Oak trees, lined Euclid Avenue. This was the
prettiest place I ever lived in and I was very happy. I quickly
made friends with Wynn, the girl who lived in the big house
in front and two brothers, Steven and David, who lived up
the street. We were the only kids around the same age and
we played together every day. When Kindergarten school

started, we rode the bus together. They were my first real friends.

After a while I started to think there was something different about me. They lived in the big houses and had shiny new cars. I lived in the back, in an upstairs garage apartment and our car was eleven years old. I didn't understand why, but Wynn's mom would call her into the house when she saw us together in the yard. And I didn't know we rented our garage apartment from her family.

I was allowed to walk to Steven and David's house and I spent a lot of time at their house. Their mom was especially nice to me and was always trying to feed me Matzo balls and other Jewish food. I didn't eat like that at home and I really enjoyed her food. She was very nice but after a while she started to ask me things like what was wrong with my mom; why didn't she ever see her. She wanted to know about Charlie and our car and did I like living in a garage apartment. I didn't know what to say; I never thought about any of these things so I asked my dad.

Charlie sat me down and with care explained things as best he could. He told me my mom had an illness and couldn't go out without him, and how I needed to check in on her and help if she needed something when he wasn't home. Then he went on to explain how some people had more money than others and that's why some had nicer houses and nicer cars. He told me if you worked you would make money but not always as much as someone else. The important thing was to work and do your best and if you were lucky, life would be good. He smiled, I smiled, and I was fine with that.

I don't know why but for some reason, within a year or so, we moved from that beautiful neighborhood in Loch Arbour to an old house located on a highway. There were no other houses around and I missed my friends and my nice surroundings. All I knew now was that I would be going to a new school and have to make new friends. I began to think things wouldn't be the same again.

This move would be the beginning of many moves and changes to come for me. As luck would have it though, no matter where we moved, I managed to stay in the same school district and was able to keep my friends. As time went on I began to realize that each time we moved, it was a step backward, going from one rented house to another and money was tight. I would dread going back to school each fall not having any new clothes. What helped me through these times was Charlie, sensing my distress, taking the time to talk with me about everything, from mom's health problems and our bills, to how work was slow and that was why he wasn't working all of the time. It made me remember back when they got married; he wore a jacket and tie all the time and now he wore work pants. I didn't ask why, I just knew things were tough and he wanted me to feel okay. He was really good at that and when he finished talking, he would smile, I would smile, and I was good, again.

Our ups and downs made us very close, with him being as much a friend as a father. He took a real interest in me and wanted to always teach me something new. I didn't always like it when he would make me practice the Morse code or learn how to read a slide rule. This had nothing to do with school but he assured me it would be good to know these things. My reward was a work bench he built for me out of pipes and wood. It was a smaller version of his and we would work together fixing things. He made me feel important and made me strong, particularly in not feeling sorry for myself. I began to analyze and assess things. Whatever I was asked to do, I did it, and never complained.

In return, I had more freedom than most kids had and I was able to get around exploring and making new friends. Every time we moved it was an adventure and I wasn't afraid to go it alone. The more I got around, the more I felt the need to do something to get what I wanted. I wanted to have what most of my friends had, nice clothes and sneakers. When I had the chance, I told my dad the truth about how I felt. Not so much about where we lived, but what could I do to earn money to help and get some nice things.

It was the summer of 1954 and my tenth birthday. Charlie said he had a special present for me and he and my mom smiled as I opened it – a custom made shine box which he had built from scratch. Charlie was working as a mechanic now back at Casino amusements in Asbury Park, so we drove to work together every day. I spent the next two summers on the boardwalk, shining shoes and selling the Asbury Park Press.

My nickels, dimes and quarters added up pretty fast. I would give him my money and he would keep a record. He would dole out the money for me to buy the nicer sneakers or jeans I wanted. Once in a while, he would use my money to pay a bill and give me an IOU, but that was okay with me. After a while, the only thing I didn't have was a nice house. It didn't bother me too much until friends wanted to know why I didn't have them over. So I just told them the truth, my mom was sick.

As I grew older I had more questions about me, my mom and my past. Charlie always took the time to carefully answer them. For example, I always knew my mom was ill but not that it was from brain damage resulting from being kicked by a horse when she was twelve. Or that Charlie grew up on a farm in Michigan and that his father would beat him so bad, he ran away to Chicago at fifteen years old and never went back. I wanted to know what happened to my real father and Charlie told me how he died from a brain hemorrhage in 1946 when I was two years old and how my mom cared for me by herself for two years after that until they met. He spared me the details then about what a prick my father was and how he used to beat my mother. I would find out more about that another day. Somehow after learning all this, I looked at my parents as never before. No matter how bad off I thought things were at times, I realized my life was nothing compared to what they had been through. I felt sorry for my mom and why she was off and on, but now I understood why. I appreciated Charlie more too knowing how dedicated he was to us. He made me want to be strong and caring like him, doing his best to take care of everyone. I was still a kid but I knew where we were as a family and I felt good. My dad would do his best and so would I. That was the beauty of my upbringing, no one bitched or complained. We just did what we had to do and that was that!

There were plenty of times as I got older when I could feel the embarrassment of being poor. Kids could be mean and I traded punches with a lot of those who made fun of me or where I lived. But I knew this was all temporary and just an ugly phase of my circumstances. I also knew that anyone making fun of me or feeling sorry for me couldn't handle what I could. I was smart and morally and mentally strong. The older I got, the better my view on life and what I wanted.

TWO
MY CHALLENGE

By the summer of 1960 I had just turned sixteen and had completed my second year at Asbury high school. We were living in Oakhurst, New Jersey and renting a two bedroom bungalow, a slight improvement over the last house we lived in a few blocks away. We were still struggling but things were better. I was getting ready to go back to my summer job washing dishes and was looking forward to the summer. By this time, Charlie insisted my friends and I call him Chas. We were growing up and he considered us adults and we thought that was cool. Everyone loved my dad...

One night over dinner, Chas dropped the 'Atomic' bomb. He proudly announced that he had bought us a house and we were moving.

"No more rent," he said with a delightful look on his face. "Wait until you see this place."

I couldn't believe this was happening, again. By this time we had moved a dozen times already, from one crappy house to another, and I never complained. I had made a lot of nice friends since childhood and now that was all going to change. Not only would I be moving twenty miles away, but I would be going to a brand new high school where I wouldn't know anyone. I'd have to start all over and the thought was unbearable.

His bomb exploded when I asked about the house only to find out it wasn't really a house at all. He tried to say it was a mobile home but I new better. It was a trailer, in a trailer park. Oh that's just great I thought. Not only do I have to make new friends but now I have the humiliation of living in a trailer. I would prefer to live in a run down shack.

We moved quickly leaving furniture and other stuff behind that we knew wouldn't fit. I was sure Chas was dodging the landlord back in Oakhurst for us to move twenty miles away. I couldn't believe my eyes when we pulled into the park. It was a gravel parking lot with about ten trailers in assorted shapes and colors. I couldn't believe ours was the first one in from the gas station and facing Highway 71. It was aluminum and looked like a train car painted sky blue and in need of a shine. It was about forty five feet long and nine feet wide. Just like a train car, it had a built in step you climbed up to open a small metal door; again, just like a train. Then I noticed the tires. Holy shit, did Chas buy this thing so he could tow it off into the night if he had to? I was too old to cry but I sure felt like it.

Once inside it was like a doll house. There was a tiny living room and a tiny kitchen with a tiny dinette set. The kitchen connected to my tiny bedroom which connected to a tiny bathroom which connected to their bedroom at the end. The passageway, a term I would become familiar with later, was about two feet wide and ran from the kitchen through my bedroom, through the bathroom and into my parents' bedroom. This meant that anyone in the living room or kitchen needing to go to the bathroom had to walk past my little bed to get there. Then, they had to remember to slide the door shut. Can you imagine that? If they had company, I had to wait until everyone left before I could go to bed. When I was in bed, I could I hear them talking in the kitchen, going to the bathroom, or talking in their bedroom, so at night, I played my radio as loud as I could. The worst part about that trailer was if you didn't slide my bedroom door and the bathroom door all the way shut, you could see into the bathroom from the living room. Can you imagine walking in with your friends and someone's in the bath room with the door open? I didn't know whether to laugh or cry when that happened.

I was really upset with my new situation but I couldn't get mad. My mom was happy and the small space was safer for her getting around. Chas was neat and orderly so it made it easy to keep things that way. But now, even at sixteen, this was going to be difficult for me. I had never moved to a new town where I didn't know anyone, let alone have to face the embarrassment of people knowing I lived in a trailer. I would just have to deal with making new friends and keeping them away from where I lived. It was summer and I knew I had to make some friends before school started.

We were now living in West Belmar, a small area across Highway 71 from Belmar, a nice beach town south of Asbury Park on the Jersey shore. My street, Eighteenth Avenue, went all the way to the beach about three miles east. Shark River was close by too which was great for fishing. A few blocks from my house there was a candy store and luncheonette called Casagrandes. It had a news stand and I always saw kids sitting out front whenever I passed by. Since I lived close by, and this was the only store around, I figured it was time to meet the guys.

I walked toward the store and as I got closer, I noticed a few evil eye stares. Shit, I thought, don't tell me I'm going to get into a fight. I tried to walk past them toward the door when the oldest kid looked at me and asked, "You live around here?"

"Yeah, I moved in a couple days ago from Oakhurst," I said waiting for a reaction.

"So where'd you go to school?" he asked. I noticed the other kids staring at me.

"Asbury Park High," I said looking him in the eye. I wasn't sure what to expect.

"Forget` Asbury," he said." You're in West Belmar now and you'll be going to Wall with the farmers," he laughed. "We just graduated Manasquan so we're done with this shit, right guys?" Two of the guys shook their heads.

"So, where do you live?" he asked.

"Over on Eighteenth Avenue," I said. I was praying he wouldn't ask exactly where. I sure as hell didn't want him or anyone else to know I lived in a trailer.

"Cool," he said. "Hey, I'm Cal. This is Billy and Bruce. We're going in the Coast Guard in August. These other two guys are Pete and McNeel; you'll be going to school with them."

"Nice to meet you guys. I'm Eddie, Eddie Spear," I said.

"Anyone ever call you Spear chucker?" Cal asked.

"Yep," I said. I didn't want to lie. That was my nickname in school.

"Hey guys, we got us a 'Spear chucker'," Cal said. Everyone laughed including me as I shook hands with everyone and headed inside the store.

"Lou, say hello to Spear chucker," Cal yelled to the guy behind the counter.

I felt relieved having been accepted and making some new friends. Cal would turn out to be my best friend for life. Unfortunately, years later his would be cut short.

During the summer we had become close. We all spent most of the weekdays going to the golf course to caddy. If we didn't get out, and on weekends, we would fish at the river or swim at the beach and hang out every night. Cal, Bruce and Billy were getting ready to leave for the Coast Guard, so we drank beer and partied hard until their last day. That left Pete, McNeel and I stuck going to the new high school. We hated it and refused to ride the school bus. If we couldn't hitch a ride with someone, we wouldn't go and cut school instead.

Pete and I lived near each other and hung around a lot. He was my first friend who I let know I lived in a trailer. He was cool with it because his house wasn't anything to rave about either. They lived in a small bungalow and he was lucky to have his own room. His mom was real nice but his step-dad was a real piece of work. His name was Bill and he was an angry bastard who was always yelling at Pete about something. I think he did this to make himself feel big because he was younger than Pete's mom and he was bald. Plus, he and Pete's mom also had a baby. Bill would go out of his way to pick on Pete, especially in front of me, over nothing and actually try and get Pete to fight. Pete was tough but would end up running out the door in frustration. He wished his step-dad would drop dead. We agreed Bill was one pissed off guy and if we could, we'd beat his ass. I felt bad for Pete. My step-dad was bald too but he was the nicest guy in the world. My friends liked him and he liked them.

McNeel had a different home situation. His parents were old, drunk, nasty and passed out most of the time. He hated them and the only time we would go to his house was when he knew his parents were drunk and passed out. We would wait outside while he would steal some money and their car keys. Then, we'd get some beer and drive off to the Pinelands. McNeel was a year older than us and would like to talk about joining the Marines. We didn't pay much attention to him though, hell, we all talked about getting away someday.

Rather then be at home, we hung out at Casagrandes. We'd listen to the juke box and if we had any extra money, we would gamble on a very special pin-ball machine. It didn't have any flippers and depending on which numbers six steel balls landed, the machine racked up points with each point being worth a penny. Casagrandes was the only place to hang out and give us a chance to make enough money for our essentials: beer, cigarettes and gas.

The owners were Lou and Diane. At thirty-five, Lou was already going bald and didn't really like us hanging out there. But that's what kids did back then and besides, he knew he made more money off of us than he paid out. Diane was a sexy knock-out who flirted with everyone who came in the store. We figured this drove him nuts which was why he was always in a bad mood. They knew each of us by name and at least once a week Lou would tell us that the store wasn't a hangout.

"If you're not spending money, you can't stay in here," he'd say and Diane would just give us a wink. During the summer we didn't care as much, but in the winter, Lou could be a real ball breaker.

Casagrandes was our meeting place. Before school we'd get up extra early so we could meet there and hitch a ride to school. After school and on the weekends there we'd be there again. It didn't matter that many of us attended different schools. Some kids went to the St. Rose and some to Wall. Every once in a while, new guys would come in and try and hang out. But unless they attended one of our schools, or lived in the neighborhood, utter mistreatment would send them packing. After all, we had to keep our little group exclusive. Lou didn't like when we did this so he would kick us out for a week as punishment. Deep down he wished he could replace us with kids who might have some real money but ultimately, this was our place and Lou and Diane knew it. West Belmar wasn't the kind of place people would move to unless they were broke.

None of us had a real job other than caddying at the golf course once in a while or shoveling snow. I actually got hired by one of the fishing boats at Shark River as a mate but got fired after two days for getting sea sick. It was a good thing too, because I hated having to be there at five in the morning. Anyway, we were always trying to scrape enough money together for cigarettes, gas and a couple containers of beer. Cigarettes were a quarter a pack and gas was a quarter a gallon. A quart of draft beer from a bar was thirty five cents.

In New Jersey, liquor stores sold packaged beer which was too expensive. Bars could sell draft beer for take-out all day until they closed, but only in a quart-sized cardboard container. It wasn't always easy for us to come up with a buck or two, so if need be, we would steal whatever change we could from Lou's news stand and McNeel would steal from his parents. Getting someone to buy it for us was easy with Khro's bar being next to the store.

Earlier in the summer before they decided to join the Coast Guard, Cal, Billy and Bruce decided we needed to form a club and we would be called the Elegants. The name came from a 50's group who had a hit song called "Little Star." So from that point on, if you didn't commit to joining the club, you couldn't hang out anymore. To be a member you had to wear the club jacket which was dark blue with your name on the front and a gold star under Elegants on the back. As I said before, everything was exclusive.

At twenty five dollars, it took a while before all of us could afford the dark blue jackets with our names on the front and the gold Elegant's star embroidered on the back. We were now the Elegants, from West Belmar, New Jersey. Not a gang so much, as a social club. Gangs were in northern New Jersey and New York City. We were just a bunch of cool guys from the Jersey shore who were different from the other kids around. We also sent a message to the kids from other towns that went to our new school: don't mess with the Elegants, and no one did.

Cal, Bruce and Billy who started the club were off in the service, so we had to carry on the club's tradition; always wear your jacket and never back down from a fight. There was no leader so we never had meetings and there was no structure. Seniority ruled and that was that. One day the oldest member of the Elegants declared himself the leader. His name was Jimmy but he liked to be called the Swan. He was the oldest and toughest guy still hanging around with us. Even the founders respected him enough to let him join the club back in the beginning. Jimmy refused to buy the jacket, preferring his black knee length leather trench coat instead. This distinguished him from everyone else and was fine with everyone else as well.

The Swan was nineteen going on twenty five. Half Irish and half Sicilian, he loved church and was good about going every Sunday. He dropped out of St. Rose high school a year or two earlier and would occasionally hang out with us at the store. He was about six feet tall and had a reputation for being the toughest guy around and a great pool player. We weren't sure how he made his money other than playing pool because he never spoke about work. To us, who knew him on a personal level, he was a real gentleman and very charming. He always had the smooth gift of gab and could pass the right compliments at the right time. He would stop by my house not knowing I was grounded and insist on coming in and talking to my dad. Next thing I knew, Chas would say "Okay, just don't be too late." It didn't matter if he was talking to a cop or your mom; he knew what to say and how to handle himself. Sometimes when we got pulled over by the cops, Jimmy would talk to them, give them our beer, and off we'd go in separate directions. Usually that worked, but not always.

Jimmy had the only car and not being in school anymore, he didn't mind driving us around. Jimmy knew what bars he could get served in so he was the beer man. Especially on weekends, we would ride around with him drinking beer. Jimmy made everyone feel that we were safe with him. Kind of like the older brother none of us ever had. On the other hand, if you crossed him or said the wrong thing, he would punch you in the mouth.

One night in the drive-in theatre I over stepped my bounds.

"So, are you banging that new chick, Kathy yet?" I asked.

Pete and McNeel started laughing from the back seat. Without saying a word, Jimmy punched me in the mouth, breaking off one of my front teeth. The car went silent. I knew better to say anything so I sat there in pain holding my broken tooth. No one said a word, and a few moments later, he put his arm around me.

"I did that for your own good," he said. "Never say anything about someone's girl, understand?"

Christ, I didn't know she was his girlfriend. But that's the way he was, unpredictable. Now that we started to hang out with him and after my episode, we were careful not to get out of line with him. To this day, every time I rub my tongue over my crown, I think of Jimmy.

Jimmy had problems at home but mostly brought on by himself. All his parents ever wanted from Jimmy were for him to become a Priest. That was why he always went to Catholic school. His father was an Irish milkman and his mom was a Sicilian housewife. Frannie, as Jimmy's mom called his dad, was always on Jimmy's back, especially since he quit St. Rose high school in his senior year. He would never acknowledge us and would always refer to Jimmy as a bum, right in front of us.

"Get a job, you bum," he would say.

One day Pete and I went into his house while Jimmy asked his mom for some money. Fran started yelling, "Get the hell out you bum!"

Marie, his loving Sicilian mother, was screaming at Frannie to "leave him alone why don't you," trying to push Jimmy away. "No more money, get a job like your father says." she screamed at him.

Pete and I stood at the door watching and listening to the screaming. As Jimmy gave them the finger and walked toward us at the door, he stopped and reached into their bird cage. In an instant, he squeezed their parakeet to death. Pete and I ran to the car while his mom and dad were screaming "Don't come back you bastard!" "I wish you were dead you good for nothing piece of shit!"

We were trying not to laugh and Jimmy told us to shut the fuck up and get in the car. I was thinking about Pete and McNeels home life, but this took the cake.

Hanging out with my friends made me realize that my home life was in fact heaven compared to theirs. Sure I was frustrated that we were poor and that my mom suffered from mental illness and that we lived in a trailer, but there was never any yelling or screaming. If Chas got upset he would use words like "disappointed," not "get out or drop dead you bastard." And believe me, by sixteen, I was no angel. We were the best of friends and we stuck together. If for some reason we had to be at someone's house it was mine. They liked my dad a lot because he was normal and the kind of dad they wished they had.

It took a while but I got used to them making fun of my house.

"Hey, this is like being on a train," Jimmy would say.

The main things we all had in common were that we weren't college material and we all hated something about our lives. Mine was just living where I did, being poor and being totally bored with school. They had good reasons to be pissed, not me. Hanging out now with Jimmy, we were all walking a fine line between good and bad; each day more toward the bad. It was only a matter of time before one or all of us got into some real trouble. We had all been taken to the police station a few times for drinking. One night we were arrested for throwing beer bottles at the car in front of us for cutting us off. Chas raised hell with me several times for having to come to the station and get me. I respected him which was why I never got any worse than this. The things we enjoyed most, drinking, smoking and loitering, weren't helping us or our self-esteem. And to add to our already degenerate ways, drugs started to appear in school.

One day, Jimmy asked us to ride with him to Asbury Park. We parked on the wrong side of the tracks and waited while he went inside a rundown apartment building. It didn't take us long to figure out he was looking for drugs. He got in the car and handed me a small paper bag.

"Put it under the seat and don't ask me shit," he said. "I'll tell you guys later".

Pete and McNeel were in the back seat. I turned and looked back at them and we all rolled our eyes. We didn't say a word.

"I'm dropping you guys off at the store. I'll be back around eight or so."

We talked outside for a while and agreed that this was how Jimmy was making his money, dealing drugs. Later that night, he picked us up and Jimmy made us swear, on our Mothers, not to tell anyone anything about him. He gave us an education regarding various pills and heroine. We watched him 'skin pop' heroine but there was nothing we could say to him without the threat of an ass-kicking. Being the good leader that he was, he threatened all of us with a beating if we dared try it. He just knew it was what he wanted to do, so we just drank our beer and kept our mouths shut. Fortunately, we never went beyond pills, particularly 'bennies' which truck drivers took to stay awake.

We tried to keep our distance from Jimmy because we didn't want to be involved if he got caught with drugs. This went on for a week or so until one night he saw us in the store and made us go out with him. We parked in the woods drinking our usual quarts of beer and smoking cigarettes. Jimmy was high on something when McNeel announced that he had signed up for the Marines. We couldn't believe it.

"You're full of shit McNeel," Jimmy said. "Your parents won't let you."

"When the fuck did I ever listen to them?" Eddie went on. "I'm out of here."

"You gotta be kidding me, what about school?" I said. "You're not going to graduate?"

"I can finish in the Marines, they have a program. Besides, I need to get on with my life," McNeel said. "You know how shitty it is, I can't even have a girl over or nothing."

Pete and I glanced at each other knowing just how he felt and what he meant.

"Why didn't you tell us you were going to do this?" I asked.

"You kidding?" he laughed. "You guys would have bitched and moaned and try to talk me out of it. I knew better and now it's done. I'm outta here!"

"Well, here's to you," Pete said, and we all took a swig of beer.

After a few parties, McNeel left for boot camp.

THREE
THE EPIPHANY

With McNeel in the Marines, Jimmy busy with drugs and Pete more distant than ever with his problems, I started to focus more on school. Coincidently, John F. Kennedy had just been elected as our new President and became the main subject of my World History class. Our teacher made him the focal point of past, present and future things to come, and getting everyone interested in what was going on in the world, in particular Berlin, Germany.

I started paying more attention to issues and discussions related to the "Cold War." Our teacher went into great detail describing how since the end of World War II fifteen years earlier, the United States had been engaged in a cold war with China and the Soviet Union over the proliferation of nuclear weapons and the global spread of communism. She explained how after the war, the Soviet Union occupied and imposed communist rule over most of Eastern Europe, including half of Germany and one quarter of the capital city of Berlin. She also described how the Chinese also adopted communism after the war, and tried, unsuccessfully, to overthrow the free democratic government of South Korea. This started the Korean War and American troops were sent along with our allies to fight the communists. I was old enough to find all of this very interesting.

I actually looked forward to this class and really got into it. I learned why our unwillingness to withdraw troops from Berlin and our criticism of communism pissed off the Russians. I learned who Premier Khrushchev was and what his threats meant to the world. Up until now, my friends and I didn't know or care about politics, but now it was clear to me. The Soviets wanted us out of Berlin, and were threatening a military showdown and nuclear war.

I found myself thinking about my friends, McNeel, Cal, Billy and Bruce, and where they were, and what they were experiencing now that they were in the service. I would watch TV with Chas, particularly the news and we would talk. He felt that we should have run the Russians out of Europe at the end of the war when we had the chance and that it was President Roosevelt's fault that we didn't. Chas had served in the Army during the war but did not see combat. He told me he tried to re-join the fight the Communists in Korea but by then he was too old. I remember he seemed apologetic when he told me that but it didn't bother me. I was more interested in knowing what the military was like in general. He said it was the best thing he ever did. He was in the signal corps and they had taught him electronics which gave him a skill that he would not have had otherwise. That made sense to me. When ever I was with Pete and Jimmy, I would want to talk about Kennedy, the Russians and what if we go to war. Their response was "Yeah, we'll kick their asses if they try anything," and that was about it.

We used to cut school a lot on Fridays and on this particular day, January 20, 1961, we were in Casagrandes. Lou had his black and white TV on behind the counter and President Kennedy was taking the presidential oath. Lou told us to shut up and listen as he began to give his inauguration speech. Everyone in the store kept quiet and glued to the TV. I remember his famous words,

"Ask not what your country can do for you; ask what you can do for your country."

No one noticed when the door opened.

"Holy shit, McNeels' here!" someone yelled.

"Hey guys, how do I look?" McNeel asked, all decked out in his green and tan Marine uniform.

"Like a soldier" I yelled as we all ran over to him hugging and shaking hands.

"Soldier my ass," he said. "I'm a Marine, Semper Fi!"

"Whatever you say man, you look great," I said grabbing my coat.

"Come on, let's go get some beers."

Everyone laughed and Lou was still shushing us as the four of us walked out to Jimmy's car.

"McNeels got shotgun," I yelled getting in the back seat.

We drove off, got what we needed and headed to our old but safe drinking spot in the Pinelands. After we shot the shit for a while, I wanted McNeel to give us all the details about what joining the Marines was like.

"So what's it like, where've you been?" I asked.

We all listened intently, even Jimmy, who popped some unknown substance with his beer. McNeel was cocked in the front seat so he could see all of us and began. He explained how he went to the Post Office in Asbury Park and saw the Marine recruiter who took care of everything. He said he forged his old man's signature for permission to join because he didn't want his parents involved. A while later he was on his way to Parris Island, South Carolina for boot camp.

"What was it like, boot camp and all," I asked.

"It was hell," he said. "Frankly, I don't know how I made it. It was all head games and physical torture and your Drill Sergeant screaming and spitting in your face. And having to say Yes drill sergeant, No drill sergeant, whether you agreed or not. From the minute you wake up you're marching, do-ing pushups and crawling in mud. At night we would march through the swamps with snakes and bugs and gators and

worst of all, sand fleas. We shot rifles and had bayonet practice and hand to hand combat. But hell, it ain't all that bad. I'm
made it back didn't I?" "Whoo Rahh" he yelled and started
laughing. We all laughed.

"Where are you going next?" Pete asked.

"I've got to go to back for advance training and then I
guess to Germany, that's where the action is," he said.

"So, Jimmy, you think I can kick your ass now?" McNeel
said teasingly.

Jimmy slowly turned, gave him the evil eye and blew a perfect smoke ring toward McNeels face. We all shared a funny
kind of laugh. A comment like that could turn into a fight.

We switched our conversation to the other guys, Cal,
Billy and Bruce and wondered how they were doing. We
hadn't seen any of them since they went in and figured they
must be on a ship or something. As far as McNeel was concerned, they were all a bunch of pussies. Marines were the
only real warriors in his book. Silently, I was thinking how
cool it would be to be like them, but more so, like McNeel
in particular. He had balls to go and join and get out of here
and on with his life.

When I went to bed that night, I couldn't stop thinking
of McNeel being a Marine. It started me thinking about my
own situation. If he could do it so could I. My seventeenth
birthday was a just few months away and I would be old
enough to join, although I would need Chas' permission. All
of a sudden I was excited at the thought of getting out on
my own. I knew McNeel was my ticket and I needed him to
stop by my house, in uniform, before he left. I thought about
Pete and Jimmy as well. Maybe we could all join and get away
from here.

I called McNeel and asked him to come by and see my
parents before he left. He said he would that Friday when

he was leaving for Parris Island. I thought about getting Pete and Jimmy to stop by too, but decided against it. I needed to do this myself; they would only be a distraction. Chas knew McNeel and liked him. I knew he would be glad to see him. More importantly, I knew he would be impressed seeing him in uniform.

McNeel showed up as promised and looked sharp as a tack. Even his shoes were shined like patent leather. Chas shook his hand so hard I thought it was going to fall off. Chas did that with everyone he met. He genuinely liked my friends and he knew the hardship of McNeels home life. My mom was having a good day and gave him a nice hug. My dad, McNeel and I sat around the dinette set and Chas poured each of us a glass of Manischewitz wine. He always had a bottle of that stuff tucked away in the fridge and surprisingly, I never thought of drinking it. Chas didn't drink hard liquor so this was as good as it was going to get. We made a toast and I watched as my dad listened intently as McNeel described his experience, although he didn't mention forging his parents signatures. I wanted to jump into the conversation a couple of times, and ask right then and there, if I could join but something told me to wait until McNeel left. After a second glass of wine, we said goodbye and he left.

"He looked great, didn't he?" I said.

"Yes he did, how old is he now?

"Well, he joined when he turned seventeen, so he's going on eighteen."

I couldn't wait any longer.

"Dad, why did you join the Army? I stated.

"Well, the war started and I felt I needed to be a part of it," he said.

"You know, they almost didn't take me because I was too old."

"What do you mean, you were too old?" I asked not knowing what he meant.

"They wanted young men, not over twenty six, and I was almost thirty. Well I made such a stink about their rules, especially in a time of war, they finally took me. I remember the guys used to call me Pops," He said.

I could tell he was thinking back in time by the smile on his face.

"You know dad, all we talk about in school is war with the Russians," I said.

"I think it's going to happen and happen soon, do you?" I asked.

"Yeah, I'm afraid I do. This thing is Europe and Berlin is getting serious."

"What's on your mind?" he said, his head turned and he looked right at me.

"Dad, I need to ask you for the biggest favor ever." I was really nervous.

He gave me a look that I had never seen before, like I was him wanting something and not knowing how to ask for it.

"Dad, I want to join the Marines," I blurted.

"Why, do you want to be like McNeel, you don't have it bad here do you?"

"No dad, I don't and that's not the reason." I said starting to feel bad.

"Really, dad, I'm going to be seventeen in a couple of months and I just feel it's my time to change things."

"What about your school, you need to graduate high school.

"Dad, I try in school, you know that, but it just isn't for me. Besides, I can get my high school GED in the Marines, just like he's doing. I swear, I will, and I'll make you and mom proud. Please dad, let me join."

I was almost crying as he poured us another glass of wine. He looked at me in his loving way and said,

"Okay, bubby, but you have to promise you'll get your diploma, right?"

"Yeah dad, I promise." I came over to him, trying not to cry, and gave him the biggest hug ever. I always knew he wanted the best for me, and this was my payback for being a good kid. I was now the happiest kid on the planet and I couldn't wait to see Jimmy and Pete and tell them my good news.

Man oh Manischewitz, oh what a wine!

FOUR
MY PLAN

Pete was home when I went to his house and we went straight to his bedroom and closed the door.

"You ain't going to believe this. Chas said I could join the Marines," I said shaking.

"You are shitting me, right? How? When? He asked with a grin on his face.

I told him how McNeel stopped by on his way back to South Carolina and we had a talk with Chas about the Marines. How after he left, I was able to convince Chas to let me join provided I got my diploma. I promised I would and that was that. Pete couldn't believe it and just kind of looked at me.

"Pete, we've got to go together, just like Cal, Billy and Bruce did. You, me and the Swan, this is our way out of here."

"What does Jimmy think?" he asked.

"I haven't seen him yet, besides, I wanted to tell you first," I said. "Come on, let's go find him."

"I can't, I have to do something with my mom when she gets home. I'll meet you guys at the store later."

"Ok, see you later. Talk to your mom before you talk to dip shit," I said on the way out.

I left and headed for the store figuring Jimmy wouldn't be at home. He never was except to sleep once in a while. Sure enough, his car was across the street and he was inside. I waved at him to come outside and when he did, I said I had something really important to tell him. I handed him my last dollar and asked him to go next door to the bar and get us a couple beers. With my dollar in hand, he didn't even ask what I wanted to tell him. When he came back with the beer, we walked behind Casagrandes so we wouldn't be seen.

"So, what's important, you knock somebody up?" he said laughing.

"Hell no, I'm joining the Marines," I said. "And you and Pete need to join too. We can go together."

I couldn't tell if he was interested or not.

"You kidding, Chas is letting you do that?"

I told him what happened when McNeel stopped by.

"Is Pete going to do it?" he asked.

"I hope so, but with or without him, you should join. Jimmy, this is our way out!"

We finished our beer and went back inside to wait for Pete. When he got there, we re-hashed everything I had told them. I maintained my position that I thought we should all go, and I made it clear, I was going with or without them.

"There's no way that prick Bill will let me join," Pete said.

"Yeah, you got a problem with that ass hole. I don't know why you haven't killed him by now! Anyway, I ain't got a problem, I can sign for myself." Jimmy said.

"Don't listen to him Pete," I said. "Let's go to the re-cruiter and get what whatever information we need, and you can deal with Bill then. Besides, pull a McNeel and forge his signature if you have to."

"No way can I do that to my mom, and besides, Bill would kill me."

We agreed to see McNeels recruiter in Asbury Park and get as much information as we could. Pete and I cut school and Jimmy picked us up at the store. It was ten miles to the recruiting office in Asbury Park and I kept reassuring them we were doing the right thing. How cool it was going to be in the Marines.

"Hey, let's just do it," I urged. "Everyone will be proud of us and we'll be outta here!"

The Post Office building in Asbury Park was an elegant structure built in the early 1930's. A few stories tall with stately columns, it was in keeping with the stature of the most prosperous major city along the Jersey shore. We had seen it before, but this was the first time any of us had been inside. There was a huge marble lobby with booths for the postal workers and tables for the customers. We looked around and found the sign for the recruiting offices. We looked at each other with renewed confidence and proceeded to climb the long winding marble steps to the second floor.

At the top of the stairs there was a long hallway with office doors across from each other. Each was dark wood with glass panels individually labeled in gold letters - ARMY, NAVY, AIR FORCE, MARINES. We checked with each other one last time and walked quickly to the door labeled Marines. We stared at the sign, "back in 15 minutes." There was no where to wait so we kind of just stood there. Then, we heard this voice behind us, "the Sarge won't be gone long, why don't you wait in here?"

We turned around and there he was, leaning in his doorway with a cigarette in one hand, and a cup of coffee in the other. I had never seen a navy Chief Petty Officer before. His uniform was distinctly different from the Marines or Army uniforms I had seen. His was more like an Admiral; someone really important. He wore a navy blue suit with a crisp, white shirt and black tie. On the top of his left sleeve, there were gold chevron stripes, and more gold stripes on his forearm. His chest was full of assorted ribbons and medals. To us, he looked to be about forty, but looking back now, he was probably no more than thirty. He offered us chairs and told us to relax and light up.

The office walls were covered with pictures of fighting ships and planes of all types. One that stuck with me the most was the biggest ship I'd ever seen, an aircraft carrier. Wow, the pictures of ships on the high seas, sailors and jet planes, all a part of the Navy image. We sat back, lit up and relaxed just as he'd suggested. "Coffee anyone?" he asked.

We couldn't stop smiling at each other. The more he talked, the more impressed we were. I was imagining the three of us in our uniforms as I listened to the Chief outline a magical, mystical tour sailing the seven seas. He said we could go to boot camp together and even be on the same ship if we wanted. The more he talked, joining the Navy made more sense than the Marines. I thought about McNeels' description of boot camp and sleeping in a ditch with snakes. I wondered if he even thought about joining the Navy. Anyway, the Marines were part of the Navy, so why would it matter. I had made my decision, I was joining the Navy.

"So boys, what do you think, are you ready to sail the seven seas?" he asked.

"Yes sir," I said without waiting for Jimmy or Pete. "I just want to make sure I can get my GED or my dad won't let me join."

"Not a problem son, I guarantee it and I'll put that in writing," he responded.

"Thanks Chief, how soon before we leave," I asked excitedly.

"Get your papers in and you'll be on your way by summer," he said with a smile.

We left with our papers in envelopes with the US Navy seal and a sworn promise to mail them back to the Chief as soon as we got our parents to sign off. We also promised to send him more fine boys just like ourselves. As we left, I avoided looking over at the Marine office. I had just joined the United States Navy, and that was that.

On the way home, we all decided the Navy was the way to go. I told Jimmy and Pete to get their papers signed and mail them back right away so we could all go the same time. They agreed and we agreed to see each other later.

As soon as I got home I showed Chas my papers. He read each form and signed where necessary. I was so excited I thought I was going to pee my pants. When he was done he looked at me.

"You're sure you want to do this?"

"Never been more sure of anything dad," I said.

We both smiled and then told my mom I was joining the Navy. She could tell I was happy so she smiled and gave me a hug. I mailed that envelope back the next day.

Now I couldn't wait to go to school the next day so I could get the papers allowing me to quit school.

Word got around that we had joined the Navy and there was a lot of excitement in school and in the neighborhood. Other kids wished they could do what we were doing, but they were either going to college or weren't old enough. By now the possibility of war with Russia was pretty well known, and everyone supported the need to stand up and fight for our country if necessary. My teachers wished me well, but they were disappointed that I was quitting school.

Every day I checked the mail and with each other to see if anyone received our "appointment for physical" notice. This was the next step in the process. After a week or so, mine arrived instructing me to report to the Armory in Newark. The Chief had said the sooner our paperwork was received and processed, the sooner we would be scheduled for physicals. When Jimmy drove me to the Armory, we pulled up to a stark looking warehouse building in an old section of Newark. Jimmy waited in the car so he could smoke and listen to the radio.

Going for your military physical is every bit as nasty and intimidating as you may have heard or could imagine. Inside, the building looked like a large gym with military pea green walls, brown linoleum floors and the smell of an old hospital ward. There were soldiers, military doctors and a bunch of guys, just like me, from all over central and northern New Jersey. It didn't matter what branch of the service you were joining, this was where you came for your military physical.

The soldiers were barking orders at everyone, "Line up side-by-side, lift your left arm and touch the shoulder of the guy next to you." Now everyone was in line and about three feet apart. The doctors and their assistants came by to ask a variety of questions, recording your answers on their clipboards. When they were done, the soldiers yelled to us, "Drop your pants, underwear and bend over and touch your toes. No talking." So there I was with fifty other guys, bent over wondering what was going on behind me. It was virtually quiet except for footsteps and an occasional chuckle from somewhere. Then it began, "You, pull your pants up and leave the room; you, pull up your pants and leave the room." What the hell was going on I wondered. I had no idea what they were talking about. This was everyone's first time taking a military physical so no one knew. Some time later I found out it was rumored that the doctors were trying to identify homosexuals. No one could verify that but after all, this was back in 1961.

It was now May and my birthday was just a few weeks away. Pete and Jimmy still hadn't received their notices for physicals and didn't seem interested in finding out why. I knew they were finking out. Sweeney was being thrown out of his house a lot and had taken up with a girlfriend. We hardly saw him any more. Pete hinted more than once that his mom didn't want him to join. Mentally, I was already gone so I didn't push them. I was in my last week of school when my papers arrived. Chas had to sign for them and had them waiting for me when I got home. Man was I happy. This was it! I was to report for induction at 1 Whitehall St., New York City, on July 12, 1961. I hugged and thanked Chas again before I ran out to find Pete and Jimmy.

We hooked up at the store and I told them my good news. Lou and Diane seemed very happy for me like they always knew I had the guts to join. As I expected, Pete and Jimmy told me why they couldn't join. Pete said his step-dad refused to sign the papers allowing him to quit school and that he was going to run away. I believed him, knowing that asshole of a step-dad he had. Jimmy was another story. He said he got a letter back from the Navy rejecting him due to his police record. That may or not have been true, but the real talk was, he was going to get married to Kathy. It was all good. We were the best of friends and there were no hard feelings. I was so ready to get out of here and on my own they could have told me they were joining and I wouldn't have cared. Finally I would be out of school and out of that damn trailer.

Jimmy, Pete and I saw each other as much as possible before it was time for me to leave. They threw a big party for me out in the Pinelands and plenty of kids showed up for the beer. There were guys from school who never bothered with me, wishing me the best. It was the same with some girls too, but at least I got some good titty and French kisses. Jimmy's girl Kathy introduced me to her girl friend, Carol, who I did remember from school. From that night until I left, she loved me like I was going off to war or something. She was gorgeous, hot and promised to write me every day. I remember thinking it was a good thing I didn't get involved with her in school, maybe I wouldn't want to be leaving now.

My day to report had arrived and Jimmy was driving me to the bus station in Asbury Park. He and the two girls waited in the car while I said good bye to my mom and dad.

"Mom, dad, I love you guys," I said crying and hugging them both.

"Take good care of yourself bubbie, make sure you write." Chas said.

"Bye son, be careful," mom said smiling. She always smiled.

"Don't worry, she'll be fine," Chas said patting me on the back.

"I know dad, thanks for everything." I hugged him as hard as I could.

I stepped out of that trailer knowing I wouldn't be back for a long time. I also knew things in my life would never be the same either. Bring it on, please.

FIVE
ANCHORS AWEIGH

I put my one carry bag with minimal clothing and essentials as instructed in Jimmy's trunk and hopped in the back seat with Carol. We kissed and fondled each other the whole ten miles to the Greyhound bus station. Wow she was hot and I was wishing I could stay another day or two. As I got on the bus, she promised to write everyday and couldn't wait to see her again in three months. Jimmy waved as they walked away to his car. I started feeling euphoric during the two hour trip to New York. I couldn't believe I was finally on my way.

I arrived at the Port Authority bus station in New York City and as I got off the bus, soldiers were yelling for me and other recruits arriving from other places to assemble by the special buses which would take us downtown to 1 Whitehall Street in lower Manhattan. There we were herded into an old skyscraper building and waited in line to be taken up elevators to a massive ball room. It was alive with men in uniform representing all the different services along with hundreds of civilians just like me. Everyone was here that day to be sworn into the Military regardless of which branch.

The walls were adorned with American flags and a huge picture of President John F. Kennedy. After a few speeches by different military personnel, order was established and at least a hundred of us were asked to raise our right hand to take the Military oath. When we got to the end of our pledge, everyone there from all over yelled, "I DO!" Right after that, there were flash bulbs everywhere. We didn't know it but this must have been a major event for the media. A year or so later, a friend showed me a copy of a newspaper from that day and there I was, on the front page in the front row with my right hand raised. It was me alright, wearing my favorite black Ban-lon shirt. The headline read something like "Young Men Rise to Meet Crisis in Berlin."

Later that day, all of us who joined the Navy were on a train from Penn Station, New York to Chicago and the Great Lakes Naval Base in Great Lakes, Illinois. The train from took about twenty four hours to get there. At least two railcars were dedicated to us, the new Navy recruits from all over the tri-state area of New York. A couple guys here and there seemed to know each other but for the most part, each of us were on our own and alone. Everyone was friendly though saying hello and wanting to know where you from and basically just making small talk. I felt the excitement of adventure this being my first time really on my own. Like me, this was the first time away from home for most of the guys. I remember standing around a bunch of guy's playing cards and watching them for hours. I never played cards so I was learning about poker from scratch.

There wasn't anything fancy about the train. We were kept to the two cars by a few sailors who accompanied us on the trip. I along with other guys wished we could talk to them but they kept to themselves. I was sure this was boring for them too baby sitting a bunch of new recruits. Along the way we ate sandwiches and drank cokes. Some of the guys wished they had smuggled some beer in their bags. I remembered the warning in our instructions that anyone caught with alcohol or dirty pictures would face punishment. Although we slept sitting up, the trip didn't seem to take as long as it did. Everyone was pumped up about our new adventure and no one complained.

It was dark when we pulled into Union Station in Chicago. I could sense authority and power all around us. Real sailors in uniform, with SP on their sleeves, were on the platform as we got off. They were yelling orders: "Make sure you have your bags, step off and form a line to your right and wait for further instructions."

We tried to follow their orders as best we could and were soon lined up to board official United States Navy buses for the drive to the naval base. It took a couple hours to get there but no one seemed to care. The bus ride was much different from the train and reality was starting to sink in. No one was talking and it was dark when we arrived at the base. Most of the guys were wide awake peering out the windows. Once we passed through the main gate, it was stop and go. It seemed like we traveled miles. Finally the buses pulled up in front of what looked like a huge airplane hanger. "Get your gear and fall out" was being shouted up and down the parade of buses. I remember the strange feeling I had watching the buses pull away. This was it, I thought, but I wasn't afraid.

Somehow we managed to line up and march into what looked like a large airplane hanger. Inside it was the size of an enclosed football field full of metal double bunk beds. There must have been hundreds of them. Most had already been occupied by recruits who arrived before. Each of us were handed a gray wool blanket and a pillow and told to stow our belongings at the foot of our bunks. There were sandwiches and cokes available on long tables for us to eat. After a while, they announced twenty minutes till lights out. The rest of the night was hell. There was a lot of moaning and some crying. I remember sleeping in my clothes and thinking about home and Carol, Jimmy and Pete. Most of all I was thinking what the hell did I get myself into?

Morning came early, around 4:30am and with a very special alarm clock. Did you ever hear a coke bottle being rubbed around the inside of a metal garbage can? Well, that's what they did while yelling "wash up and fall out in 10 minutes." Fortunately there were large bathrooms with sinks and toilets for all of us.

It was still dark when we went outside and huddled into groups so we could march to the mess hall. Imagine learning to march in the dark and with people yelling at you for stepping on their feet. Meanwhile everyone is being told to shut up and stay in step. It was very confusing to say the least. What the hell does keep in step mean and why are my ears still ringing from that coke bottle routine?

The mess hall was another new experience. Inside you sat at long metal tables and waited until your table was called to get in the food line. Here was where you picked up a metal tray and silverware and proceeded to the serving area. The metal trays were uniquely designed with each indent sized for portion control. There was a large indent for an entrée and smaller indents for sides, roll and desert. As you proceeded down the line, food was ladled onto your tray. At the end of the line there was the standard issue white coffee cup used for milk, coffee or the most common beverage, "bug juice," which was really strong Kool-Aid. Just like the coffee, bug juice would stain your cup making you wonder what it might be doing to your stomach. A big sign behind the cooks said, "TAKE WHAT YOU WANT, BUT EAT WHAT YOU TAKE." This meant when you were done, your tray better be empty.

The Navy has nicknames for certain food items. For example if the breakfast menu said ground beef in red sauce on toast, it was called "red shit on a shingle" or "Red SOS." Ground beef in white sauce on toast was called "white shit on a shingle" or "White SOS." And chipped beef in cream sauce on toast was called "Foreskins on toast". If the lunch menu had bologna, they called it "Horse Cock". Once in a while they would serve something special like steak and eggs or meatloaf which was considered to be normal food and as such, had no nick name. This was Navy food, and would be my food for what would seem like the rest of time. Rumor too was that all the food in boot camp contained "salt peter," which was a drug that would reduce our libido and prevent us from getting horny for the next three months.

By the time we were done with breakfast, it was light out and the march back to the hanger was somewhat easier. Within a short while, it was fall out and line up again. This time we marched to the base barber shop. Here, everyone had their hair cut as close to the scalp as possible, making all of us look stupid and unrecognizable. This was the Navy's way of bringing all recruits down to the same level and making all of us equal. No pretty boys here. And that was just the beginning. Next, it was off to get our Navy issue clothing.

Off we marched to another warehouse building and one by one proceeded through an assembly line similar to that at the mess hall. As I went from station to station I was handed an item, the first being the standard navy sea bag. When it is folded you have no idea how much stuff it can hold; everything but your pea coat. I filled it with socks, underwear, bell bottom jeans, denim work shirts, blue work hat, blue work coat, two sets of white uniforms - one dress and one regular; two sets of blue uniforms - one dress and one regular; one black scarf, two white sailor hats, one navy 'flat hat,' two pair of black work boots, two pair black dress shoes, two belts: one blue and one white, and two brass belt buckles. The funny thing was, no matter what size you told them, you got something bigger. All you heard was "keep moving." Last but not least, I got the traditional Navy pea coat, which by now would not fit into my sea bag. At the end, we were each wearing our pea coats and lugging our massive stuffed sea bag of clothes in the July heat to the next location. Here we would be issued personalized cardboard stencils cut out with our last name, initial and serial number, and two tubes of special laundry proof paint - one black and one white. We were told to stencil our names on every item of clothing and to write our names on the inside of our shoes when we got settled in our permanent barracks.

As of today it was official. We were now government property, belonging to the United States Navy. Carrying our sea bags full of new clothes, we marched back in the heat to the hanger we had arrived at the day before to retrieve our belongings, and then to head off to what would be our new home for the next three months, Camp Moffett.

We must have marched for an hour before we arrived at a large complex of identical one story bungalows. Each had a wooden sign on the front and side to identify one from the other. Ours said Company B, for Bravo Company, and that was what we would be referred to from now on. We even had a flag, navy blue with gold Company B in big letters. Inside the barracks, there were two private rooms on each side – one for the Company Commander and one for his assistant. As we proceeded inside, it opened into what looked like a giant "A"-frame building with nothing but double tier bunk beds on each side of the room. At the rear of the building there was an exit and to the left, a giant shower area connected to an open toilet and urinal facility, which was connected to another open area of sinks. No privacy for anyone whatsoever. Its one thing to pee next to a guy but it's entirely something else to take a dump next to someone. Hell, we didn't even know each other at this point. Awkwardly, each of us paired up and claimed our upper or lower rack and locker choices. We didn't have much time to settle down and stow our gear from our sea bag to our lockers before evening mess, so everyone was scrambling around.

"Attention on deck!" someone yelled out of the blue.

Everyone froze not knowing what to do, but instinct told us to stand up straight and shut up. Slowly the Company Commander, the "CC," and his assistant the Assistant Company Commander, the "ACC," came into the main bunk area. They walked by looking at each of us not saying a word for what seemed like eternity. It was so quiet and tense you could hear a pin drop. Then very calmly they introduced themselves as Chief Petty Officer Andrews, the CC, and his assistant, First Class Petty Officer Peele. The Chief wore the same uniform as the guy who recruited me. Peele wore the same sailor uniform as us; however he had three chevron stripes on his arm signifying he had the rank of a First Class petty officer, one level below Chief.

The Chief asked each of us, one by one, to state our names and where we were from. When the last guy finished, he told us he didn't give a shit.

"Your sorry asses belong to me and Peele now and we will make sailors out of you. If any of you screw up, the whole company will be punished, do you understand?" he yelled.

"You will make Company B the best graduating class the Great Lakes Naval training center has ever seen. Do you understand?" he yelled again.

"Yes sir," everyone yelled out of sequence.

"You will acknowledge with Aye, aye sir. Do you understand?" he screamed.

"Aye, aye sir," we yelled.

"Now stow your gear, put on your work uniforms and fall out in fifteen minutes," Chief Andrews said.

"Aye, aye sir," we yelled again as they left.

We all began to introduce ourselves while they stood outside the front door smoking. "Fall out for mess hall in three minutes or no one gets to eat." Peele yelled in from the front door.

We were dressed and outside in a flash. I looked around at everyone and realized how ridiculous we all must look in our baggy clothes, but hey, this was part of the humbling and humiliation process. Everyone's clothes were either too big or too tight. Work hats were either too big or too small. The only thing that seemed to fit right was our shoes. I guess even the Navy figured out our feet were the most important part of our body as we marched off to the mess hall.

Inside were mostly recruits from other companies, but there were some regular sailors stationed at the base there as well. I could see them looking at us and laughing as we came in. Some guys took offence to their snickers, but they knew better than to act up. I was just glad there were plenty of other new recruits there so we weren't the only goofy looking guys.

After chow and back at the barracks, Peele told us the smoking lamp was lit, meaning we could smoke in a special area, until lights out at 10pm. He also reminded us how Chief Andrews could give a shit about us, and if we wanted to make it, that he was the day-to-day boss.

"You got that, you faggot pollywogs?"

"Aye, aye First Class Petty Officer Peele, sir" we said.

"Just call me boss when the Chief isn't around, got it?" he said. "Otherwise, its first class petty officer Peele."

"Aye, aye Boss sir!" we responded.

After he left, we had a chance to stand around and bullshit getting to know each other better. We agreed he was a good guy and to watch out for the Chief. Some guys were already cussing out the Navy and some were already questioning if they were going to make it. I remember counseling some of my new friends that night. I told them, hell, we only have three months of this shit. Let's make sure we work together and don't fuck up. I wasn't worried after all I grew up pitching in and doing what I was asked to do all my life.

The next day was the calm before the storm. It was day two and we marched off to the post office. We bought stamps and envelopes and then got to go to the "Ships Store." Basically it was like a department store full of Navy items including stationary, notions, candy and things you might want to send home. It was relaxing to be there and it gave us a chance to use the pay phones to call home and let everyone know we made it to boot camp. Every call ended with "I don't know when I can call you again, but I will write and send you my address." A lot of guys had tears in their eyes after hanging up. Back at the barracks, we all knew today was special and that tomorrow would be the beginning of a new life experience and we wouldn't be calling home again for a long time.

Over the next couple of weeks, some of the guys were getting homesick. I could hear them sob at night after lights out. Others would go berserk when they got their "Dear John" letter from their girlfriend who by now was getting lonely and wanted them to know they had taken up with some one else, probably their best friend. I never worried about it. I was getting love letters from Carol every other day. On the outside of the envelope flap, she would write: "I'm jealous of the United States Navy," and it would smell of perfume. My friends were in awe of my letters and pictures of her and how beautiful she was. I would let them sniff her fine perfume.

One day her letter looked different. I looked at the flap and read "Feelings have changed." I immediately smelled it;

uh oh, no perfume. I knew something was up so I started to laugh and invited everyone over so I could read it out loud.

"Dear Eddie, I'm sorry but I can't wait three months to see you again. Mickey has asked me to go back with him and wants me to go to the same college with him. So that's what I am going to do. Good Luck, Carol."

The guys were silent and I pretended to cry holding my eyes. When they weren't expecting it, I started singing Neil Sedaka:

Oh Carol, I am such a fool,

Darling I love you, though you treat me cruel,

You hurt me, and you make me cry,

But if you leave me, I will surely die

Darling there will never be another...

They guys didn't say anything not knowing if I was serious or not.

"Bullshit, I yelled. "There are plenty of broads, just wait until we get out of boot camp! Screw you Carol, I wasn't looking for a girlfriend anyway!"

The guys cracked up. I thought it too bad that other guys couldn't handle their 'dear john' letters as well as I did. Every week from now on, there would be many more to come. A few guys took it so hard they left and we never saw them again. I found my new shipmates helped me confirm and expand my view of things, especially women.

We were from all over this side of the Mississippi; north, south and mid-west America. I found fascinating the fact that our personalities and opinions were sometimes different about things including girls and relationships, growing up at home, why we joined, just about any topic of discussion. I learned quickly there was a big difference between northerners and southerners and to tread lightly on certain matters, like race, the civil war and Governor Wallace. This was common sense and it was one of the secrets of getting along in the military.

Company B started out rough like every new company of recruits trying to fall in line. Chief Andrews and the boss stayed on top of our performance to mold us into what they knew we had to be. Sometimes, someone would talk in line and we'd lose our place for chow or someone would fail inspection and we'd all have to scrub the barracks, but it all worked out. After the screw ups realized they were ruining it for the rest of us, things got better. We fell in line and started to walk the walk with few problems. Every day except Sunday would be the same routine for the next three months. Wake up to the coke bottle scraping the garbage can and fall out for personal inspection. March to the mess hall for breakfast and back. Fall out for calisthenics and physical training followed by more marching, then the mess hall for lunch followed by cleaning the barracks and getting ready for inspection. Back to the mess hall for dinner, and then back to the barracks to shower up and relax. Lights out at 10pm and start all over again the next day.

Morning personal inspection was the worst part of boot camp. You stood at attention with your white hat turned inside out, hanging on your index finger. You flip the inside of your tee shirt collar out. Chief Andrews and Peele would stand in front of each of us one by one, staring, and if there was any sign of grime on your hat where it touches your head or on your tee shirt where the fray rubs your neck, you were in deep shit. Your shirt and pants are wrinkle free and your boots spit-shined. Your body is frozen and your eyes are fixed in a straight forward stare. God forbid anyone move or make eye contact with the CC or the boss who are looking us up and down just waiting for someone to flinch. If too many individuals fail inspection, the whole company will be scrubbing the bathroom with a toothbrush for the next eight hours. Remember, in the Navy, cleanliness is next to Godliness.

By the end of two months, the entire company was a hundred percent in sync. We marched in precision and were physically and mentally different from when we arrived. We were now, according to our boss and the CC, ready to learn what the Navy was really about - training for duty aboard ship. Less time was now being devoted to marching and physical fitness and more time for testing to determine which skills we have that may best fit the Navy. You did not have any say in what duty you would be assigned; the Navy tells you based on a barrage of tests and interviews

There were more and more days of classes and testing including: psychological, hearing, sight, and special aptitude. Most of the time you didn't understand the questions so you just marked which box you thought was correct. Near the end of boot camp, you found out what it all meant and what you were going to be doing. I was very fortunate. When I was a kid my dad taught me basic electricity, how to read a slide rule and the Morse code. Though I didn't realize it then, I had learned something very important, Dots ••• and Dashes • • • the main form of communication between ships. During the battery of tests it was apparent that I knew Morse code, and unknown to me at that time, my destiny was to be a Radioman. This was a very special skill and would pay off duty wise compared to many other sailors.

SIX
CINDERELLA LIBERTY

We had reached the end of our tenth week in boot camp. At this point, with only two weeks left, we were granted Cinderella liberty. This meant that Company B, and other companies who had completed ten weeks of basic training, were allowed to leave the base on Saturday morning but had to be back on base by midnight. We had to decide where to go with such a short timeframe. Some of the guys chose to go to Waukegan because it was closer, but as for me, I was going to Chicago, a couple hours away. So a bunch of us took off for 'Chi-town' as it was called. We boarded a train and were headed downtown to Union Station, the same station I arrived at from New York ten weeks earlier.

Chicago was a huge city, second only to New York, and with the Great Lakes Naval Base just on the outskirts, it was also a Navy town. This made it easy to figure out where to go and have some fun. State Street was the main drag then, and was known for its bars and Burlesque shows. None of us were twenty one so we settled on Burlesque. Most of us didn't know what that was but we were up for it after ten weeks in boot camp.

"Come in sailors and relax," the barkers standing in front of each theatre would yell.

We picked one and paid three dollars to get in, which was a lot for us. But we were sailors, on liberty and horny too. Plus, we had just drawn our first pay so we all had at least forty bucks.

The place looked like an old movie theatre with a stage and a couple hundred red velvet seats occupied by a couple hundred sailors in their crisp, oversized white uniforms. The girls were hefty with big tits and had their nipples covered with red tassels. This must be what they mean by burlesque, I thought. Some were dancing in a group to a rag time band and others were dancing by themselves to a piano. That was just fine for a bunch of horny teenagers like us who hadn't seen any woman for months.

"Take it off, take it off," guys were yelling from the audience. Some guys were even throwing their white hats up to the stage so the girls could rub them in their crotch, kiss them with their red lipstick, and throw them back. Fights almost broke out as everyone wanted to sniff those hats. For us, it was a really fun time. I'll tell you for a fact that salt peter stuff doesn't work.

After our fill of watching tits bouncing and hips grinding, we left to have some fun. We started looking around for someone to buy us a bottle of booze. Sure the Navy warned us about the consequences should we be caught drinking or under the influence, but we figured it was still early and we had enough time to sober up. Besides, we agreed after what we'd been through the past ten weeks, and seeing those girls, we deserved a drink. It was definitely worth the risk.

It wasn't hard to find a liquor store or a bum to buy us a bottle and some beer. A dollar for the bum, a beer for each of us, plus a bottle of bourbon to pass around, was just what we needed. We slipped into a nearby alley and stood out of site of the street and sidewalk. Lighting up, we began to pass the bottle around. I didn't have too much experience with hard liquor, and bourbon wasn't the right drink for me. I could hardly get it down, much to the amusement of a couple southern boys. We were careful not to get caught drinking, or to get our 'whites' dirty, so we stayed in the alley for quite a while. We laughed about everything from boot camp to the old broads we had just seen in Burlesque. Although we were from all over the states, we got along just fine outside the barracks. All of a sudden, every kid I met in my life so far didn't matter as much as these guys. This was my first experience with the meaning of camaraderie, and it gave me a nice feeling. I really liked the Navy.

Time was going by quickly, and by now it was time to get something to eat and hopefully find some girls. Soda pop, pizza and burgers, we couldn't get enough after eating nothing but SOS, FOT and Horse cock for the past two and a half months. There were girls around but they didn't want anything to do with us recruits. They were interested in plenty of other sailors who were senior to us and stationed at the base. Getting lucky would not be in the cards for us on this trip, so we spent the rest of our time walking back to the station, taking in the sights of the Wrigley Building and Michigan Avenue. It was great just to be out on our own for the first time as sailors. We were closer than ever as friends and we made sure everyone got on the train together.

We had heard all about Cinderella Liberty; if you weren't in by midnight, your ass was grass! You would have an extended stay in boot camp and you wouldn't like it one bit. We all made it back with no trouble and our night out gave us plenty to laugh about safely back at Camp Moffett.

SEVEN
REAL NAVY TRAINING

Our final two weeks of boot camp had finally arrived and we weren't dumb recruits any more. It was now time to learn the real part of being a sailor, like how to fire a pistol and a rifle; how to fight a ship fire and how to jump into burning water and swim with your clothes on. We would practice this daily bringing our twelve weeks of naval training to a conclusion. We were anxious, raring to go and nervous as hell at the same time.

The rifle range was awesome. We learned how to fire a .45 caliber pistol and the infamous M-1 rifle in the standing, kneeling and lying down positions. For me and most of the other guys, it was the first time we had ever fired a gun. They didn't give us ear plugs, so after my turn my ears were ringing. I figured if you are firing at the enemy, you don't have time to think about ear plugs. A few of our guys were country boys and hit the targets dead on. These were the same guys who insisted we drink bourbon that night on liberty. Later, they would all receive medals for sharp shooting.

They don't give you a swimming test to join the Navy, but you will learn to swim or stay in boot camp until you do. Growing up on the Jersey shore, this wasn't a problem for me; I had been swimming all my life. Fully dressed in our work clothes, I along with everyone else, had to climb a thirty foot tower. When it was my turn, I was instructed to cross my chest with each arm and jump straight down, feet together. When I surfaced I had to swim like hell away from the tower and burning water. Oh yeah, they throw some stinky fuel on top and light it just to give you a chance to swim under water a while to avoid the flames on top. To top things off, one of the drills was to swim pulling another sailor to safety. Even as good as I was, jumping off that 30 foot tower into the water with my clothes and shoes on, was pretty damn scary. I remember a few of guys were so scared they actually refused at the beginning and only gave in when they were threatened with a 'less than honorable' discharge from the Navy.

Even without fire, swimming with your clothes on is no easy feat. This is why the Navy uniform has a specific purpose in its design. Specifically, the white sailor hat and the bell bottom pants can help you float in the water. Once wet, your hat can be used to scoop in air and submerge it in the water in front of you. This acts as a flotation device as long as you keep it wet and keep scooping. The bell bottom pants allow you to easily remove them with your shoes on. Once off, you can tie the end of each pant leg in a knot. Once tied and wet, the pants can be used to scoop air into them. By tucking each air filled leg under your armpits, you can use them as a flotation device as well.

Fighting and surviving a fire onboard ship was another experience. A fire is the worst thing that can happen, and as a result, our training was intense to say the least. Everyone goes through basic fire training since it is assumed, that sooner or later during your enlistment, you will serve aboard ship.

Every day we marched to a large field which had several metal structures resembling a ship's compartment with 'wheel lock' hatch doors. Basically, each was about four hundred square feet with one entry door. We were each given a Navy issue flashlight and a gas mask. One by one, we entered the dark compartment and sat on bench seats. When we were all inside the door was closed and secured. We sat there silent, in this very dim lit room, waiting for something to happen. Suddenly, there was a boom and everything went black. Within minutes, the ceiling started to glow red, and it started to get hot.

Flames started to trickle in, from a far wall, and our visibility was getting bad to the point where we couldn't see anything.

A voice came over the sound system giving us basic instructions: turn on our flashlights, remain calm, don our gas masks, and help the person next to us if necessary. Find the fire extinguishers and proceed to put out the fire. Open the bulk head doors only when the fire is completely out. Remember to cover our hands with our shirt before opening the hatch, as it will be hot. We did this every day for a week before we graduated, just to make sure we had it right. And, that is how serious the Navy is about training for a fire aboard ship.

EIGHT
GRADUATION

Boot camp was finally over and it was time to graduate. The day before, Chief and the boss congratulated us and presented us with our new stripes to signify our graduation from boot camp and a promotion from Seaman Recruit to Seaman Apprentice. After the normal breakfast routine, we were back in our barracks sewing our new stripes onto the left sleeve of our dress Navy Blue uniforms. It was now October and the Navy had shifted from 'whites' to 'blues' in this part of the country, as the Uniform of the Day. We would wear our Dress Blues with our new stripes to graduation ceremonies.

The next morning we didn't get the garbage can wake up call. Instead, the boss came in yelling.

"All right sailors drop you cocks and grab your sox! Fall out for your last chow as Seaman Recruits, you got one hour." He barked.

It was a very special day and every one was happy, snapping bath towels and having a good old time. Outside it was a beautiful October day, around sixty degrees, with blue sky. We marched to the mess hall and as we went in all the regular recruits, still in boot camp clothes, looked at us with envy. They knew by our dress blues and two stripes that we were graduating today. I remember us all laughing and having a good time. One of the guys who always thought I was funny was sitting across from me. I told one of my many made up stories and waited until he took a sip of his milk before I delivered the punch line. As predicted, the milk shot out of his nose much to the amusement of everyone. He wiped his face and just kept laughing. We all got along really well.

Back at the barracks it was the final tune up for spit shined shoes and perfect square knots in our scarves. Pretty soon it was fallout for assembly at which time Company B lined up in formation for the march to the parade grounds.

"Ah-ten-hut!" For-ward, March!" Chief Andrews yelled.

As we marched with our company flag carried in front, we fell in behind Company A who would lead the way. Behind us, Company C and the other graduating companies would fall in as well.

I didn't have the opportunity to graduate high school and participate in graduation ceremonies, but I don't think that could compare to mine. Five hundred highly trained sailors marching in precision with all the protocol, fanfare, pomp and circumstance of the military and the Navy band. I will never forget my pride that day and the special feeling of accomplishment. I thought how impressive it must have been for the friends and family who attended to see all the many companies - A, B, C, etc., marching past the gallery of Admirals, Captains and other officers. We marched in per-fect step, eyes fixed straight ahead as we approached the viewing stand.

"Eyes Right, Salute!" Chief Andrews shouted.

In one perfect move, all of us snapped our heads to the right and held a salute with our right hands until the gallery returned our salute, acknowledging their approval for our ability to now serve and carry on the Navy tradition.

Later, we were seated along with friends and family and listened to speeches about the history of the Navy and our global role in world freedom. How we controlled the seas with the largest fleet of ships and aircraft in the world and how important we were in these times of the Berlin crisis and a possible war with the Russians.

As the ceremonies came to an end, the Navy's Blue Angels flew over the crowd after which we were ordered to stand:

"Attention on deck!"

The band played 'The Navy Hymn," and after what seemed like ten minutes, the words we had long been waiting to hear:

"Dis-missed!"

A few hundred hats flew into the air.

What seemed like an eternity had come to an end. The first three months of my new life experience was over. I had completed boot camp, the first and most important challenge in my life, and it made me feel great. I did it on my own. From joining and getting on that train to Chicago, it was all about me. I wished my mom and dad could have been here to see me graduate, but that was okay. Showing up at home in uniform would be enough. I knew how proud they would be and it made me buzz inside.

We had all made it except for a few sorry asses who couldn't adapt to military life. They ruined it for us in the beginning when everyone was punished for one person's screwing up, but it didn't take long for the boss to get on to them. They were sent home as undesirable for military service.

There was nothing to do now except pack. We were now regular Navy and had free reign of the base. I went to the PX with some friends to buy the final Navy souvenirs, coffee cup; plaque, and some post cards. The phones were so busy there I didn't even try to call home. I figured I would just show up and surprise mom and dad. This was our time to relax while we waiting for our orders. Some of us would go to ships and others to shore duty somewhere. We were all anxious as hell to find out.

Finally, Chief Petty Officer Andrews and First Class Petty Officer Peele came into the barracks to personally congratulate each one of us with the highest compliment to a sailor: 'Job Well Done. They also had our orders in hand so a hush came over the barracks, as they called out names in alphabetical order, last name first. At last my name came up.

"Spear, Edward!"

"Here sir," I replied.

"Radio School, Bainbridge, Maryland, report in two weeks."

"Aye, Aye Sir!" I said as I felt my pants getting wet.

Oh my God I thought, thanks to Chas teaching me the Morse code, I was being rewarded with a nine month shore duty assignment just four hours from home. I thought back to how much I hated having him quiz me, and make me practice over and over, and for what? All the other guys seemed happy with their assignments to ships, air fields, hospitals or for further training. I was the only person assigned Radio school.

Before we left, most of us exchanged phone numbers, addresses and promised to keep in touch. I was surprised that the navy provided bus transportation back to Chicago. A lot of us ended up at Union Station Chicago, where we were on liberty just a couple of weeks ago, and where we arrived three months earlier not even knowing each other. But this time we were different. We were friends and men serving in the US Navy.

NINE
AHOY MATES

I was more excited to be heading home now as I was when I left. I was me now, not Eddie Spear, the seventeen year old kid just hanging out in West Belmar. On my own I made the choice to take responsibility for me. I was now Spear, Edward, Seaman Apprentice, United States Navy. I was proud to be traveling in my dress blues. Back in 1961, all military had to travel in uniform. The Navy paid for my transportation home and to my new base, however only by bus or train. They didn't pay to fly anyone, so I took the train and arrived at Penn Station New York, where I had departed from three months earlier.

I was waiting for the train to Belmar when a couple of business men stopped and insisted I join them for a beer in the commuter bar located in the station. The drinking age in New York then was eighteen, and even though I wasn't there yet, bellying up to the bar in my dress blue uniform and sea bag didn't cause a problem with the bartender. And buying me a couple of beers was typical of New Yorkers showing their appreciation that I gave a shit about what was going on in the world and had the balls to join the service. Two months earlier, the Russians constructed the Berlin wall and a threat of war was worse than ever. I realized being in the service was very popular now and everyone was friendly. This new experience of traveling alone, Penn Station, and drinking with strangers who appreciated me as a sailor, was different from anything I ever experienced before. Automatically, I felt and acted older and more confident like never before in my life.

It was late in the day when my train, The North Jersey Coast, left for the Jersey shore. There were a lot of business men onboard heading home after a busy day in the City, particularly on Wall Street. The ride to Belmar would take a couple of hours with a fifteen minute stop for the electric engine which left New York to switch to diesel. It would take years before the shore line would be electrified like the main line between New York and Philadelphia or Chicago.

I lugged my sea bag through the crowded train. I got plenty of friendly looks and smiles from some really cute girls but the seats were full. Finally, I made it to the bar car where I found plenty of room for me and my sea bag. God that thing felt like it weighed a hundred pounds. I sat down and made my self comfortable.

"Hey sailor, come have a drink with us," some guys yelled from the bar.

I walked over to a group of men in suits, some looking only a few years older than me, standing at the bar. I was the only military man and everyone was insisting I have a drink with them. The bartender who worked for the railroad insisted on seeing my ID so I said I'd have a coke and went back to my seat. The car was crowded with men drinking and smoking. Before I knew it, several cans of beer appeared on the table in front of me. Looking around, I saw the guys raising their glasses my way as a toast. Damn, I was feeling really good. Twenty years later, I would be a commuter riding this same train, in the bar car, on my way to and from the City. Nothing would change over that period except for new faces and me wearing a suit.

The train finally pulled into Belmar and I took a taxi to the trailer a few miles away. The cabbie told me no charge so I thanked him and insisted he take a couple of bucks as a tip. I walked around the back of the gas station and peered through the end window of that trailer. There was Chas and my mom sitting at the dinette set watching the TV which was on top of the refrigerator. Red Skelton was on and I could see them smiling over their cups of coffee. I tapped on the metal front door and stood to the side so I wouldn't be seen when the door opened. Sure enough, Chas looked out and not seeing anyone started to close the door.

"Ahoy Mate!" I said.

I thought he was going to fall out the front door. He grabbed my hand and pulled me and my sea bag inside. As he hugged me, I was looking at my mom, sitting there with a big smile on her face. I never told them when I was coming home so this was a complete surprise. This was the first time ever I felt happy coming home to that trailer.

My mom stayed seated while I bent over and hugged her for what seemed like ten minutes. It was getting late so my dad took her to their bedroom and came back. I stayed in my uniform the whole night watching him looking me over and over. As was the case with McNeel, he wanted to know every detail of boot camp from the day I left until now. I couldn't wait to fill him in but first I needed to know something.

"Dad, you got any of that Manischewitz wine?

"Yep, but I got a few Rolling Rocks too. Which would you like?"

"I like the wine, like we had with McNeel. It brings back good memories," I said.

We talked all night until it was getting light out. He told me how good I looked and how proud he and my mom were of me. I told him how happy I was and that if it wasn't for him, I'd be a fuck-up. He laughed.

Chas looked at me admirably and listened intently as I described every moment of boot camp. I remember he especially enjoyed my description of Cinderella liberty and our time in Chicago. He couldn't believe State Street hadn't changed since he left there back in the Forties. We talked until four in the morning. I was exhausted and finally talked my self out so I slid that compartment door open and crashed on my tiny bed. That night was the best sleep I ever had on that bed.

I slept late and when I woke up, Chas was off to work or something. I didn't remember asking how he was doing. Mom and I had breakfast after which she assured me she was fine so I headed out to Casagrandes. I was wearing my 'civvies' now, jeans, sweatshirt and sneakers. My hair was shorter and I had lost some weight which accounted for Lou not recognizing me when I walked in. His wife recognized me though, and came out from behind the counter and gave me a hug. Damn, Diane smelled good I thought.

"Eddie, you're back. How long has it been?" she asked.

"Oh, a few months I guess.

I saw Lou glaring at me; he didn't like Diane hugging anyone.

"Hey Lou, how's it going?"

"Okay, welcome home Eddie. How long you gonna be around?" Lou asked.

"Not sure, a week or so then off to Bainbridge Maryland. Hey, have you seen any of the guys?

I didn't tell anyone I was coming back so I could surprise them.

"Not lately, you wanna use the phone?"

"Thanks," I said and dialed Jimmy's number.

Jimmy came by and said he hadn't seen Pete for quite a while so our first stop was the South End Tavern. This is where we would go and watch Jimmy play pool. Lou the bartender didn't want us there but Jimmy threatened him and that was that. Jimmy would slide us a beer once in a while when Lou was busy. This was not a classy place and many times Jimmy would have to threaten the guys he played against to pay him. He was really good at setting people up for the big win. It had been a long time since I was last there and Lou was actually glad to see me and wanted to know where I'd been.

"In the Navy Lou," I said. "I just got back from boot camp."

"Well, here you go Eddie, have one on me," he said sliding me a beer.

Jimmy made sure his drink was free too!

We looked around for Pete who now had a girl friend and wasn't spending much time at home or around the store. Pete's mom said he and his girl friend spent too much time together and she hardly got to see him. Yeah, I thought, if I had his dick head father, I'd be spending all my time with her too. McNeel and Cal were gone so I wasn't going to hang at the store with no one around. After a couple of days, things started to get boring. I was totally dependent on Jimmy for transportation. After a couple of bar nights with just me and him, he started showing up with his girl, Kathy, the one who had introduced me to Carol.

"Hey, if you guys want to park, great, but drop me off." I said the second night.

"No way man, we're a three-some, right Kathy? We'll get some beer and light up."

So, that's what we did a couple of nights. Kathy offered to contact Carol for me but I decided against it.

"Thanks Kathy, but once burned, once learned." I said chugging my beer.

She did fix me up a couple of times, but all her friends knew about me and the fact I wouldn't be staying around. I'm sure they knew I was only after one thing too because it was touchy feely and that was it.

Although it had only been three months since I left, I realized I had changed upstairs and things wouldn't be the same. For one thing, my physical and mental conditioning made me feel superior and I had a hard time sharing the same small talk with Jimmy or anyone else around. Small talk, like how's it going or you look so good or where have you been, was a chore. Except for Jimmy, everyone else was gone, having joined the service or off to college. I ran into a couple of girls I knew from school and they were both pregnant probably by some dirt bags as neither one was engaged or married. What a couple of losers I thought, but that's how quickly things change when you leave and then come back. I began to move coming home again to the bottom of the list of things I wanted to do with my time. I almost didn't last the two weeks at home. I hated that trailer more now than when I was in school. It didn't have anything to do with mom or dad; it was I didn't have room for anything. I was beyond that environment for ever and I knew it.

Growing up I never had a routine other than school, but now my life had changed. I was getting restless and missing the Navy way of life. It was time to get back to my new friends who I had something in common with and get on with my life. So after just a week at home, I was ready to report to Bainbridge early. I was packing my civilian clothes to bring with me to my new base when my best friend Cal came by.

Cal had just come home on leave from the Coast Guard and Lou, from Casagrandes, told him I was home too. Cal brought some beer with him so we waited for Chas to get home from work. Cal was a couple years older than me and loved to talk with Chas. He was truly interested in Chas's knowledge of everything. I didn't get it but they really clicked, and Chas liked him a lot too. Sure enough, Chas walked in and almost shook Cal's hand off his arm, as was his custom, much to my enjoyment. We sat around and talked over a couple of beers and I told mom and dad I was staying at Cal's house and would see them before I left. That was fine. Chas new I was too old now for that bedroom.

Cal and I stopped and got more beer and headed to his house. I hadn't seen him for over a year and we had a lot of catching up to do. His mom and dad were just as glad to see me as was I to see them. They set me up in the spare bedroom with a nice, big bed. When I first moved to West Belmar, Cal was the first guy to become my friend and stand up for me in the neighborhood. It was nice to meet him and the other guys that day I went to Casagrandes, but there were plenty of other guys around who I needed to get along with. Cal made sure no one gave me a hard time and no one did. I got along with everyone anyway. It was just my personality; I was funny and easy going. I never had a friend yet who didn't appreciate that about me. Cal and I had a lot of good times before he joined the Coast Guard and we had a lot of catching up to do. It was good that Jimmy was busy with Kathy because Cal and Jimmy didn't really hang with each other. I liked them both in different ways so now it was me and Cal. My final week home Cal and I tore up the town going to all the hot spots from Belmar to Ortley Beach, further south.

When it was time for me to leave, Cal insisted on driving me the four hours to my new base. His girlfriend invited her friend Inez to take the ride with us. We stopped by my house and I said goodbye to mom and dad and reminded them I was only four hours away. I really wasn't sure when I would be back but I didn't want them to worry. I needed to keep my options open as to where I was going to stay when I came home. That trailer was out of the question.

We piled into Cal's Studebaker PowerHawk and took off. Just like the old days, we drove the Jersey turnpike south, drinking, smoking, laughing and mugging it up as best we could. Inez, was from Czechoslovakia or somewhere like that, and was hot with blonde hair and blue eyes. Now I was changing my mind about not coming back for a long time; I knew I wanted to see her again.

We arrived at my base outside Port Deposit and Cal and I said goodbye. We hugged and promised to keep in touch through his mom. I told Inez I was crazy about her and would see her again as soon as I got settled. She kissed me really hard. In reality though, I couldn't wait to get through the gate, check in and get settled.

TEN
RADIO WAVES

When I received my orders I didn't know there was more to being stationed at Bainbridge than being closer to home. No one told me that in addition to Radio school, Bainbridge was also boot camp for the Navy's female sailors called 'WAVES' Women Accepted for Voluntary Emergency Services. As it turned out, my new base had five times more women than men. This was indeed paradise after the Great Lakes.

The base was much smaller by far than Great Lakes and was located on the Susquehanna River. This was the real Navy with nice housing, shops, movies, basketball courts even a private boat house. There were the traditional barracks for the recruits, but where I lived, it was more like apartment buildings. I shared a room with another Radioman named Murray. He was already into his sixth week of school. Our room was set up with two single beds, closets and two desks. It even had a window air conditioning unit. Each building had a lounge with TV, real bathrooms and showers with privacy, and a small kitchen. This was a regular naval base with a mess hall serving regular food on real plates. No more red or white S.O.S. or F.O.T. for us. I was off every weekend but had to be back by midnight on Sunday. There was nothing really required other than go to class and keep our barracks clean. An alarm clock replaced the garbage can and coke bottle. No more marching for us either. We got to walk wherever we were going. Classes were Monday through Friday and that was it. Man, was this great.

Radio school classes were interesting and challenging. Every letter in the alphabet and number from zero to nine correlated to a unique assignment of dots and/or dashes. As an example the letter A, was dot dash; B, was dash dot dot dot; C, was dash dot dash dot and one, was dot dash dash dash dash. We were required to memorize the code and translate what we thought we heard. In addition, we had to learn how to type. To learn this, we would look at a giant typewriter keyboard on a screen and strike the key on our typewriters as directed on the screen, like follow the bouncing ball.

In the early weeks, listening to code and learning to type were separate exercises, but as time went on, we would type what we heard. That was how it was with every day, the same routine with a test at the end of each day for accuracy and speed. As we improved we were required to be faster and the pressure began to build. The receiving code was coming in faster a lot harder to be accurate. Typing on the screen was faster too. We now had to wear headsets and listen and type each letter to a beat keeping up with the rhythm. Talk about pressure. I really got into it though because it was a challenge and I was good at it. Chas had done his job.

It wasn't too long before we had another requirement to master while continuing to improve our proficiency on the message receiving side. Up until now, we learned how to listen to dots and dashes and convert them into letters and numbers. Now, we had to learn to convert letters and numbers into dots and dashes and transmit them accurately and with speed. We had to learn how to use a transmitter 'key' to send dots and dashes. In order to send code, we had to learn how to tap a spring loaded key relay so when pressed down, held and released correctly, the contact would close; when let go, the spring would open the closure. A quick tap would send a short tone, or a dot; a firmer, longer tap would send a longer tone, or a dash. Then it was all about rhythm with pauses between words. This was a very sophisticated technique that everyone had to master otherwise the message could be not be properly interpreted or misunderstood on the receiving end which could be very serious. I thought this must be what it is like to learn how to play a piano. Every day we were being tested on two things – how fast can you receive and how fast can you send. All things considered, I did pretty well. I found memorizing and converting code was easier than learning to type a minimum of forty words a minute and transmit messages at a minimum of forty words per minute but that was why we were selected to be here. We had the potential to send and receive messages accurately and as fast as humanly possible and the Navy knew that. As the weeks went on, more guys and a couple of gals were dropped and reassigned duty somewhere else.

Our time out of class was great. No matter where we went, there were regular Navy personnel, male and female. Once in a while we would pass recruits marching and exercising just like we did in boot camp. We were on alert not to whistle or get caught staring at the Waves or recruits. It was rumored that the Navy had a charge called 'visual rape' and it could get you into tons of trouble. So we would look at the recruits, they would smile and we would wink at them and they would wink back. It was fun and sooner or later, we would get to dance with them. Social life was good too because at the EM club, there were plenty of regular Waves to drink and dance with.

Every third Saturday was dance night and the best time on base. Each month there would be a graduating class of Wave recruits and as a reward, they were allowed to go to the EM club for a very closely supervised dance. This was our chance to dance with the horniest woman on the planet. We complained that they didn't play enough slow songs but what the hell, we only needed a few dances the way they locked onto you. Talk about a bear hug. We were pretty creative spiking drinks with half-pints of liquor we snuck in and were rewarded with stolen French kisses and a feel whenever possible. I get goose bumps just thinking about those dances.

My time at radio school was truly a blast. I guess it was like being in college whereby you go to class each day with the same people. Everyone got along, especially the single guys, and on the weekends we would go to all the big cities - Baltimore, D.C., Philadelphia and even to some dances in Lancaster, Pa. The girls there were fun but nothing like the recruits.

I went home once during school and it was a nightmare. I knew I had four days off, and being only four hours away, I would give it a go. I was missing Inez and I didn't have the money to get there so after talking to a couple of guys who had done it, I decided to hitch hike.

'Interstate 95,' was nothing then like it is today. I had to make my way from Port Deposit, Maryland to North Baltimore where I would take the Chesapeake Bay Ferry. Somehow I ended on the last ferry boat and there weren't many vehicles on board. After asking every trucker and car driver on board for a ride, no one was going more than twenty miles further north except for a bus headed for New York City. I had two choices: sneak on the bus and hope for the best or get off the ferry and wait all night for the next one to come over in the morning.

The driver and most of the passengers were upstairs on the main deck or in the restaurant. I went all the way to a rear seat next to a window and slunk down as far as I could. When I woke up, we were at a bus stop diner in Delaware. The bus driver was poking me.

"Can I see your ticket son?" he asked.

I was half asleep and searching my pockets trying to think of what to say.

"I don't know what happened to my stub sir, but I got on in Baltimore, one way to New York City," I said.

"That's right sir, he did get on in Baltimore," the lady across from me said.

He looked at me and walked back to the front of the bus. I looked at the lady and she smiled.

"Thanks a lot," I said feeling kind of creepy.

The next time I woke up we were on the New Jersey Turnpike just south of exit eight where I new I needed to get off or I would end up sixty miles further north in New York City. As we got closer, I worked my way up to the driver and asked if he would kindly stop and let me off. He told me it was against company rules but he did it anyway. He glared at me and I thanked him. He knew I was a stowaway. It took a couple of hours but I ended up hitching a ride the thirty miles east to West Belmar. In fact, the guy insisted on driving me to my door. Thank God for my Navy uniform. All in all, that trip took about seven hours, and I had been lucky. That was the last time I would hitch hike again. Inez was surprised when I called her. That was the way I liked it, to surprise people. We loved it up for two days. I didn't even think of Pete, Jimmy or Calvin. When I was ready to go back, Chas gave me enough money for bus fare. I was hoping he would, after all, since boot camp I had been sending him a few bucks each month. What a good son.

School was coming to an end and we were all looking forward to receiving our orders. We knew as Radiomen we could be assigned anywhere in the world. Most of us were hoping for sea duty aboard a ship. With so many naval bases around the world, land duty was a possibility as well, including Alaska or Antarctica, God forbid. Finally, our day came. We received our certifications as Radiomen and our insignias, small patches with lightening bolts or 'sparks' as they were called, on white and blue cloth. These were to be sewn above our stripes and would identify our specialty skill. I couldn't believe at the end of school I could type sixty words a minute and transmit messages at the same speed.

My orders were to report to the USS Saratoga, CVA-60 which in navy designation means, 'attack air craft carrier.' The "Sara" as she was called, was the second of the latest and largest carriers in the Navy. Over time, there would be ten 'Forrestal' class carriers like her. She was temporarily located at the Norfolk, Virginia Navy shipyard for repairs and I was to report for duty in two weeks. This was a dream come true as I remembered seeing a picture of this ship with the big number 60 on her bridge tower super-structure. The Saratoga was the ship I saw in the Navy recruiter's office almost a year ago to the day. It was ironic that I got the Sara, some of the guys got carriers as well and some of the guys got shore assignments but no one got Alaska or Antarctica which was good. We packed up our sea bags, said goodbye and headed home for a well deserved leave before reporting to our new assignments.

ELEVEN
RED SLY IN MORNING

There is an old saying in the Navy, "Red sky in morning, Sailor take warning." We were getting closer to a war with Russia over missiles in Cuba.

I hitched a ride home from Bainbridge with a couple of shipmates who were from New York. When we got to the city, they dropped me at Penn Station for my train to Belmar. I figured I had about an hour before the train so I found the commuter bar in the station where I was the previous October. It was now July, nine months later and nothing had changed; it was full of people sitting and standing at the bar. I looked around to see where I could fit my sea bag and squeeze in for a beer.

"Hey sailor, over here; come on guys, move over," an older businessman said.

"Thanks," I said setting my bag down. I ordered a Knickerbocker beer.

"John, put his beers on our tab. So what do you think of these Russian bastards and this shit with Castro? You Navy guys are gonna kick their asses, right?" he asked.

"Damn straight we will, and God bless America." I said as we all raised our glasses. I had a couple of more beers and made it to the North Jersey Coast train.

It was late July of 1962 and things had really heated up with the Russians. Fidel Castro had made a deal with Khrushchev and the Soviets for protection from an invasion of Cuba by the United States. He was going to allow Russia to install missiles capable of carrying nuclear warheads. This was in response to our failed Bay of Pigs invasion back in April 1961. Castro blamed President Kennedy and the CIA for attempting to overthrow him and his Communist regime. In July, our government found out the Soviet Union had begun missile shipments to Cuba. While the transport of missiles to Cuba was being denied by Castro and the Russians, Kennedy was making it clear the United States was prepared to go to war if any missiles were installed. Our military was already on high alert in Europe following the construction by the Russians of the Berlin Wall in August 1961 and now Cuba was becoming the real hotspot.

When I arrived home I was hoping Cal would be on leave so I would have a place to stay instead of that damn trailer. I loved mom and dad, but I was a sailor now and I had no privacy in my own house. Unfortunately, Cal's mom said he was on duty somewhere and wouldn't be home. I didn't even think of Pete or Jimmy. I immediately got on the phone and called Inez. It was a good thing I saw her that long week-end a while back. We had a great time and I knew she would be happy to see me. Lucky for me she was home and agreed to pick me up. I told mom and dad I was going to stay at Cal's and would check in with them later. That was fine with them. While waiting for Inez, I filled Chas and my mom in on my experience in Radio school. Chas was delighted, especially when he saw my 'sparks' insignia. He reminded me with a smile how his teaching me the Morse code was a good thing. That was an understatement.

Inez took me to her house and introduced me to her mother. Her father had passed away so it was just Inez and her mom. Damn, she was just as pretty as her daughter. She smiled and in a heavy accent, told me to make myself comfortable. It must have been my uniform or maybe the prospect that I might want to marry her daughter some day, which made her mom invite me to stay at their house. I enjoyed staying there and with her mom working, Inez and I had some real quality time. But after a few dinners and movies, I told Inez I needed to leave. Things were heating up and I needed to get to my ship. She was so sweet she didn't even complain. She stopped by the trailer so I could say goodbye to my parents telling them I needed to get to my ship. When she dropped me at the bus station, I told her I loved her and would write. She was really sweet and I made a mental note to make sure I married a foreign girl. I never did see Pete or Jimmy and figured I would catch them later. I headed out early, anxious to get to the USS Saratoga, in Norfolk, Virginia.

TWELVE
USS SARATOGA CVA-60

I was excited as hell when I arrived at the Norfolk Naval Base main gate. Marine guards with guns were all over the place inspecting every piece of documentation in my package before making a phone call to check my legitimacy. I wasn't sure what was going on but it turned out they called my ship to have someone pick me up. It took a while but finally a sailor in denims arrived in a United States Navy pick up truck and welcomed me aboard. He threw my sea bag in the back and off we drove for a mile or so passing buildings and streets. This was a big change from Bainbridge. There were sailors, marines and civilian workers all over the base. Finally I could see the silhouette of ships. As we approached the docks, there were more ships in sight than you could imagine. Carriers, battleships, destroyers and cruisers were everywhere.

The driver wished me luck and dropped me at the main gang plank leading up from street level to the main deck. All I could hear was noise from the workers, who were called yard birds, working on the bottom of the ship eighty feet below, and the ships loud speaker making announcements in navy speak, a whistle followed by 'now hear this!' The 'Sara' as she was called, was in dry dock for repairs. I stood there in awe staring at the size of this ship. She was as long as the Empire State building and ten stories tall from top to bottom. An aircraft carrier on water is huge, but unbelievable when you see one on blocks in a hole a hundred and fifty feet deep and a quarter of a mile long.

I lugged my sea bag over my shoulder and hiked to the top of the gang plank. I came to attention, saluted the American flag, and then saluted the Officer of the Day.

"Request permission to come aboard sir?" I asked.

"Permission granted, let me have your orders."

I set my sea bag down and handed him my orders. He looked at them and handed them to another sailor.

"Please escort radioman Spear to his quarters."

"Aye, aye sir," replied the sailor.

"Come and follow me. Keep to the right and watch your step," he said. We walked through passageway after passageway passing sailors all along the way. We went up to higher deck levels finally arriving at the berthing compartments for CR division. On board a ship, all personnel are assigned to divisions depicting their specialty. My division was CR, and stood for Communications Radio.

I met some of the guys and shown to my bunk. It was one of three high, consisting of a metal platform with a foam mattress with storage under the mattress and in two horizontal lockers built on the side against the bulkhead. My new home was the top bunk reserved for the 'new guys.' I would get to move after I moved up through the ranks.

There were fifty five of us with different ranks from seaman apprentice to Chief Petty Officer and our bunks and sleeping areas were assigned according to rank and seniority. Over the next few days, my shipmates provided me with an informal tour of the largest maze of passage ways and multi-level decks you could imagine. Picture three football fields laid out with sleeping quarters for enlisted and officer personnel, working areas, dining areas, recreation rooms, hospital rooms, not including access to ordinance, engine rooms, boilers, etc. Now, multiply this by seven levels deep and realize you are accommodating five thousand sailors and a company of marines. After a few days, I attended a formal all day guided tour along with fifty other new arrivals to the ship. Even with that, it took me quite a while to figure exactly where places were and the quickest way to get there.

All personnel on board the ship are referred to as 'ships company' except for the air squadrons' personnel; they were referred to as "air dales." They are only on board during active readiness and deployment. Otherwise they reside on naval air bases, along with their aircraft and pilots, anywhere in the US. Being a sailor on a ship is not the same as being on a base. You have duties above and beyond your designated skill. For example, everyone has an assigned battle station, which if you are not on duty, you must post when called. My battle station was to be at a certain area and lock down the doors thus sealing off that particular area. I had a headset so I could communicate with the people in charge. Others may handle fire hoses or man the ordinance stations. In essence, everyone has an assigned task when battle stations are called. Another general duty task was keeping the entire ship clean. To do this, every division on board rotates their personnel for cleaning duty assignments. Twice a day there will be a general announcement:

"Sweepers, man your brooms, clean sweep down, fore, aft and amid-ships."

That meant for assigned personnel through out the ship, to start cleaning.

The Saratoga had a central radio room and several auxiliary radio and transmitter rooms to handle inbound and outbound communications between her, other ships and land bases around the world. Communications were in the form of Morse code, teletype and single side band voice. Radio Central was manned 24/7 usually on eight hour shifts.

My job was receiving and sending Morse code messages; others guys were responsible for teletype and cryptology messages. Radio central was the in and outs of what was happening. As radiomen, we were the first to know what was going on.

Liberty was granted to go off base during the working days and on weekends depending on our work schedule. In port, we worked eight hour shifts so after that you had your own time. I still wasn't twenty one but Norfolk was a huge base and the Navy provided a club for enlisted men and for officers. If you were eighteen, you could drink 3.2 beers. It was real beer but made special with less alcohol. That was good enough for us because you had to drink so much to get drunk, you would get sick first, usually before you could get into any trouble. Downtown Norfolk was the same except we could also drink wine. It was the wine that got us all tattooed one night. Hell, we didn't care, that made us official. I ended up with a navy anchor on one arm and a panther head on the other. Damn that Norfolk and East Granby Street.

Chicago had State Street and Norfolk had East Granby Street with its share of bars, burlesque theatres and plenty of bums to buy you a bottle. By this time however, Go-Go bars were starting to appear featuring younger, prettier girls dancing to modern music dressed in bikinis and cowboy boots. This was a major improvement over the older Burlesque scene. We would go when we could afford to and managed to stay out of trouble probably because we had a year of Navy life under our belts already. Everyone with common sense knew you really didn't want to get in trouble in the military. So, while in port, especially Norfolk, we behaved and spent more time on the ship than off.

THIRTEEN
HOME PORT

Home port can be any city on the East or West coast with deep water.

It was mid-September, our repairs were complete and it was time to leave Norfolk and head to our home port at Mayport, Florida. The base was located just east of Jacksonville where the John River and Atlantic Ocean come together. Similar to Norfolk, Mayport is home to a large contingent of Navy ships. We were one of three aircraft carriers ported there as well as several escort warships and supply ships as part of the sixth fleet.

Earlier when the Sara was on her way to dry dock for repairs, the aircraft and air squadron support personnel returned to their respective Naval Air Stations They would stay at their home bases with their families until we were again ready for sea duty. Now that we were, a thousand more sailors began to arrive on board. These were the sailors who supported the ninety aircraft and various flight squadrons which would join us out at sea. I was in the real Navy now and going to sea for the first time in my life!

As we prepared to leave Norfolk on that September morning, I along with all off duty personnel lined the flight deck on the port side parallel to the dock. This was the custom when leaving or entering a port any where in the world. Sailors and marines waved goodbye to loved ones on the dock. Ten tug boats guided us from the dock and out the Chesapeake Bay channels toward the Atlantic. As we got further away all hands were dismissed. We were now at sea and it was time to get to work and experience the real Navy.

Once out at sea our air craft squadrons started to arrive. First the sea going helicopters used for air and sea rescue followed by the prop planes used for mail and transport back to land. This went on all day with planes being taking down on elevators below to the hanger deck. Last to arrive were the jet squadrons basically in order by size and type. There were fighters, fighter bombers and heavier bombers consisting of A-3 Sky Hawks, A-6's, and F-4 Phantoms and F-8 Crusaders to name a few. By the time all the squadrons were on board, we had around ninety aircraft secured and ready for heavy weather ahead.

When we left Norfolk, we headed east and into some pretty rough seas. Even as one of the largest ships in the Navy, the Sara was pitching and heaving slowly and we could feel the unusual motion. For me and some of the other guys, this was our first time at sea, and getting sea sick would be part of the tradition. Even with all the planes on board, the ship was rolling in some very heavy seas.

The senior guys were called 'salts' meaning they had cruised on the Sara before. First timers, like us, were called 'pollywogs.' They told us that if we thought this was bad, wait until later when we cross the Atlantic to the Mediterranean. According to them, it would be so rough that we would have to be tied in our chairs with buckets between our legs, so we could keep sending and typing messages. That wouldn't be for a few months so we had to wait to see if what they said was true.

The Sara took her time cruising to Mayport so the air squadrons could practice take- offs and landings. The pilots get rusty being on land for too long and air ops allows them to get back into the groove of taking off and landing on a 'postage stamp' in the middle of the ocean. It was like being at a non stop airport that went on day and night.

Rarely could you see what was happening, you just heard the screaming engines and boom of the catapult when a plane was launched.

The central radio room was located in the forward part of the ship and our sleeping quarters were as far forward as you could get. In fact, we were actually only one deck below the flight deck and the catapults used to launch aircraft. There are two forward catapults or 'cats' as they are called which act like steam driven steel sling shots that can propel a jet from 0 to 120 mph in a just few seconds. When they come to a stop over our space, there is a boom and you can feel the front of the ship move. These were noises you had to get used to or you couldn't sleep. After a while being at sea, with the ship slowly rolling, you sleep like a baby.

After a week at sea, the order of the day was to prepare for arrival Mayport. The ship had loud speakers all over the ship and announcements were made over what was called the 'IMC,' this way everyone could hear orders and announcements from the Bridge. Prior to general announcements, and to get the crews attention, the Boatswains Mate would blow his whistle and announce "Now hear this" followed by whatever it was to be said. This time it was "All off duty personnel, man the rail in full dress uniform at 0800." So as we approached our home port, the thousand foot ship was once again lined with sailors and marines of all ranks.

Tug boats and fire boats were stationed with fountains of water pumping into the air and horns blowing waiting to escort us to our dock. This was a traditional maritime salute to our arrival. As we got closer to the dock, you could hear the Navy band playing Anchors Aweigh and a thousand people on the dock cheering. For many of them, these were families getting together after many months of being separated. For me and my new friends who joined the Sara in

Norfolk, this would be our new home port for the next couple of years.

It didn't take long to settle into our new routine. With the ship in port, it was like having a job. You worked eight hours and all you had to know was when your next eight hour shift was, otherwise you were free to sleep or leave the ship. Radiomen somehow were a privileged rank and I am not sure why but I think it was because there were too few of us in the Navy. It was like we got special treatment. Most other sailors had to report for work duty usually in the mess hall or cleaning or painting the ship or mopping floors. We only had to take care of our sleeping area and do what we were trained to do - receive and send messages. We were out almost every day or night exploring the general area. First, the base and the PX for shopping and the Enlisted Men's Club for food and 3.2 beers. A few of the guys who had been on the ship for a while, had cars on base and we were anxious to explore our new home area.

No matter whom you met or worked with, everyone was a wild teenager at heart, yet feeling the pull of military responsibility. Some of the guys were from Chicago, Louisville, Richmond, Baltimore and even Los Angeles. I got along with most everyone, and made buddies with a couple guys from New Jersey and New York. A couple of guys had there cars on base. Occasionally I had a chance to ride around, look for girls and drink beer, just like we did at home. Nothing changes other than you are with new special friends, called shipmates.

One day Kirby, who had a car, invited some of us to check out St. Augustine, a town about an hour away. Being a Friday night he figured we would be away from the crowded competition around Mayport and find some action there. So we loaded up with some beer and headed out, six guys in a '57 Buick just having a good time. As we drove around it turned out the whole city was nothing but houses along the beach. We were getting frustrated and as soon as we could, we reloaded with more beer and a bottle. We started driving again and I was sitting in the back seat between two other guys. The bottle of 'Old Crow' was being passed around and chased with a beer. Everyone was talking, laughing and having a good old time. After a while, I noticed the guy in the front shotgun seat was rolling his head from side to side. I knew that was not a good sign and I was on guard as I watched him try to roll down his window and stick his head out a two inch opening. I quickly ducked forward as far as I could knowing he was going to barf and it would land in the back seat. Sure enough, it blew back in and landed on the guy on my right. Kirby started yelling and pulled over. All four doors flew open and we got out of the car as quickly as we could. Most of us were laughing but a couple of guys wanted to fight, especially Kirby. Everyone cooled off and we got back in the car.

"Hey, pass me a beer," someone said and we all started drinking again.

We were laughing again and then it happened. Kirby drifted the car smack into a lamp post. The guy next to me, who got barfed on earlier, smacked his nose into the front seat and had a bloody nose. We all stood around the car bitching, laughing and looking at the lamp post laying on the ground trying to figure out what had happened. Then the cops pulled up.

"You fellows alright?" one of them asked.

"Yep" we replied. Kirby explained how he dropped his cigarette and ran off the road trying to pick it up.

"Ok, well ya'll just follow us to the station so we can straighten this out" they said.

We had our civilian clothes on so when they checked our Navy ID's they cut us a break. They didn't even accuse us of drinking even though DUI didn't really exist back then. Hell, Florida even had drive through liquor stores where they would make you a drink on the spot. Anyway, they gave Kirby a ticket for destruction of city property and let us go, however, with our complete understanding that if he didn't show up for court, we would all be arrested for property damage in the amount of $500. It was a good thing there were six of us to chip in because no sailor has that kind of money. I guess St. Augustine being the oldest city in the country had the oldest lamp posts too. Back at the ship we laughed about that night for some time and counted our blessings that we didn't get in trouble with the Navy. That would come later.

FOURTEEN
WAR GAMES

Military readiness is what it's all about with the Navy, especially in times like this with increased tensions between Russia, Cuba and the US. After returning from Norfolk, we had been in port for a while so it was now time for the Saratoga, and her task force of ships, to head out and prove our combat readiness. As was always the case leaving port, we lined the flight deck waving goodbye to those on the dock. This time we were allowed to be in our work uniforms. In no time we were at sea and totally out of sight of land and joined up with the other ships. We were heading to the waters around the USNS at Roosevelt Roads, Puerto Rico. The Navy had a base there and owned an island nearby which was used for bomb practice missions. For a week we would be conducting flight operations, bombing targets, hiding from submarines trying to sink us, and protecting our ship from pretend enemy planes and other ships. It was non-stop 24/7 launch and land aircraft and man your 'battle stations' drills.

The radio room was busy from the moment we left. There were Russian ships in the area on their way to Cuba, and we were instructed to do our best to copy any code coming from non US ships. The huge volume of messages we processed tested our accuracy and speed as Radioman. It was nothing school or being in port could condition you for.

The Sara performed very well during her critique so our reward for the war games was a two day stop in Ponce, the second largest city in Puerto Rico. For us new guys, this was our first real liberty outside the US, and we were psyched. We dressed in our crisp white uniforms, had money in our pockets and went off looking for some fun. When it was our turn, we walked down the gang-plank and boarded the liberty launch boat for the ride to shore. The boat was full and you needed to be careful and not step on each others spit-shined shoes. This was another first for us pollywogs, being shuttled by boat from our ship to the landing. Even though we were in port, the Saratoga still had to anchor in the harbor instead of mooring at the docks like the rest of the ships. This was the rule for carriers while in foreign ports and was established after the attack on Pearl Harbor in 1941. In the event of an emergency, carriers need to get underway fast.

We went ashore and it didn't take long to realize we had no clue what people were saying in Spanish. We wandered around taking pictures and taking in the sights. I couldn't compare Ponce to any place I had seen before because I had never seen a city like this in the US. This was definitely another country, in the Caribbean, so I pictured this must be what Spain and Mexico are like. We soon realized we were being ripped off on prices for everything: tours, souvenirs, even beer. So by the time the bar girls showed up wanting drinks, we didn't have any money left. Back at the ship, we all agreed:

'Join the Navy and see the World.'

Soon, we were underway again, this time for a quick stop at the Roosevelt Roads Naval base on our way back to Mayport. Again, we were able to have a quick liberty but since it was a base, we could wear our work clothes. This would give everyone a chance to shop at the PX or "ships store" as the Navy called it. There were no women or civilians stationed here just sailors and marines. There was no town or city just the base and once inside we headed straight for the Enlisted Men's Club. It was located at the top of a steep, grassy hill and looked like an old two story mansion.

I could feel the steep climb up the dirt driveway in my legs and in my chest, the result of smoking too many Camel cigarettes. Inside, the place was huge and they served real beer and drinks. Everything was cheap; a rum and coke was a quarter. After all, this place was for the fighting men of the Navy and Marines. The bartenders were local natives who could care less how old we were. They were just glad to get a tip.

We were some of first to arrive at the club. As more of our escort ships came into port, their sailors made there way to the club as well. Pretty soon, it was packed and hard to get a drink. And then the fight started. Someone said something about someone or their ship, like "what are you looking at" or "the Bradley sucks" and that's what usually sets things off. All you can do at this point is keep your eye on the guy next to you, to make sure he's not going to hit you, and avoid the swinging batons of the Shore Patrol; the Navy's version of Military Police. They have the unpleasant duty of breaking up fights, knowing they can spread like a fever, with everyone wanting to get in on the act. Before you know it the clubs are swinging.

The fights didn't involve us so we worked our way out of there and headed back toward the ship. As we were making our way down the path, new guys were coming up on their way to the club. Half way down the hill, we came across one of our shipmates who could barely walk. He was a scrawny little guy and was drunk as a skunk. We knew we had to get him down the hill, and back to the ship, so two of the guys each took an arm and started carrying him down the hill when 'bam,' some drunk with another group coming up the hill, decided to sucker punch this poor bastard in the mouth, knocking out his false teeth. We tried to catch the guy who hit him but they took off and it was more important to find our shipmates' navy issued dentures and not let him be seen bloodied by the Shore Patrol.

What a night that was but certainly a good lesson on what to watch out for when there are too many sailors drinking and no woman around. It was great to be back on the ship, underway and back to work. We were heading home now and back to normal in port duties.

FIFTEEN
ON THE BRINK OF NUCLEAR WAR

It was late September 1962 when we arrived in Mayport from our war games. Earlier that month, satellite photos confirmed the construction of military missile launch sites in Cuba with missiles in place and aimed at the United States. Russia and Cuba denied their intent and Russia maintained they had the right to protect Cuba from any invasion by the United States. This was not acceptable to the United States or the United Nations, but despite this, Russia refused and continued to bring in more missiles by ship. The whole world was afraid the United States and Russia were on the brink of a nuclear War. In fact, not since the Berlin crisis in 1960, and the construction of the Berlin Wall by the Soviets in 1961, were we this close to war with Russia. The Soviets wanted to establish a permanent foothold in Cuba. Russia and Cuba continued to deny the United States allegations and by October 8th, our military around the world was on full alert.

On October 22nd, 1962, President Kennedy addressed the world on live television and radio concerning the "Crisis in Cuba" and the threat of war. During his speech he made the position of the United States very clear:

"It shall be the policy of this nation to regard any nuclear missile launched from Cuba against any nation in the Western hemisphere as an attack on the United States, requiring a full retaliatory response upon the Soviet Union."

"To halt this offensive buildup, a strict quarantine on all offensive military equipment under shipment to Cuba is being initiated. All ships of any kind bound for Cuba from whatever nation and port will, if found to contain cargoes of offensive weapons, be turned back. This quarantine will be extended, if needed, to other types of cargo and carriers. We are not at this time, however, denying the necessities of life as the Soviets attempted to do in their Berlin blockade of 1949."

President Kennedy immediately put into place a naval blockade, but referred to it as a 'quarantine,' knowing the term 'navel blockade' could have been construed as an act of war, and that was not what we wanted. The intent of the quarantine was to stop and search any ship, Soviet or otherwise, and prevent their entry to Cuba should they be transporting any offensive weapons. In response to our President, our Navy immediately dispatched an armada of various warships into the International waters surrounding Cuba.

Even though we were back in Mayport, the radio room was busier than we had ever been, monitoring all kinds of communications traffic. Our job was to listen and capture every message we heard, especially Russian, and alert our communications officer immediately. It was obvious that Russian war ships were in the area we found ourselves scared and excited at the same time. Who would have thought things could escalate to this point in a mere two months.

One day secret messages starting coming in encrypted. Each word was comprised of only five charters making it impossible to understand. Unless you had the 'key ciphers,' which were kept in a safe, you could never understand the message. The radio room was buzzing and after a while, one of our friendlier officers said:

"Guess what guys, we're going to Cuba."

The Saratoga would be part of an increase in war ships to be located just off the coast of Cuba. We would be joining the existing task force on station. It was an odd feeling to know important information before others know, but that was why we had Secret clearances; we could not tell what we knew. Everyone would be told, but we were always first to know. After hearing our hero, President Kennedy speak that day, we all agreed this Cuba thing could be it. I remember talking with the guys about how we hid under our desk in school to protect ourselves in case of the 'Atomic' bomb.

"Duck and cover," I mimicked laughing.

There were a few chuckles but no one laughed. The thought of heading into the start of a nuclear war and Armageddon was numbing.

It was now late October and there wasn't time for local friends and family to plan a big sendoff. We got underway within twenty four hours of our orders and headed full steam to Cuba. We left port on high alert and our Captain announced the seriousness of our mission giving each of us a chill. Our Communication officers reminded each and every one of us how important it was for us to be attentive to listen and capture any strange communication coming from non US Navy ships. Duty onboard the ship had changed and everyone took on a more subdued seriousness about themselves. We were now working twelve hour shifts instead of eight. There was a real cockiness felt by all, not the usual relaxed feeling, passing others in the passageways or eating in the galley. Everyone was focused and very much on the alert. Within one day at sea, we were called to 'general quarters' and we could hear the launch of aircraft.

'Gong – gong – gong - gong

General quarters – general quarters

All hands man your battle stations

General quarters – general quarters'

It was pretty nerve wracking because you didn't know whether it was a drill or the real thing. You went to your battle stations as fast as you could get there. Lives and the safety of the ship depended on everyone doing exactly what they were trained to do without thinking. When secure from 'battle stations' was announced my friends and I would sneak out onto the catwalk which ran parallel to the flight deck. From there we could see the planes loaded with weapons of all types taking off and landing. We weren't supposed to be there and we had to stoop really low during a launch. For us this was a major rush and exciting as hell.

Being at sea at full readiness and working twelve hour shifts, you are so busy or tired you begin to lose track of the days. One morning early in the 'am' my mates and I on duty were paralyzed. The ship was called to GQ but this time it was for real.

'General quarters – this is not a drill, repeat, this is not a drill

All hands man your battle stations

This is not a drill, repeat, this is not a drill'

Holy Shit, this is it! We were yelling and an officer was yelling, 'knock it off.' We were locked down in radio central, about twenty of us including officers, nervously performing our jobs. All we could hear were jets taking off one after the other. We figured they were on their way to bomb Cuba or something. We were expecting to hear gun fire or bombs exploding but that never happened. We typed messages and tapped out messages so fast we didn't have time to read them. It was dead quiet and my adrenalin had kicked in. I don't remember how long we were at GQ but finally, we heard

"Secure From Battle Stations"

Whatever it was, it was over. No explosion, no bright flashes followed by incineration, just the words, secure from battle stations. No one knew what was going on or if anything happened anywhere. There were no 'plain English' messages to suggest any military action. All we knew was that whatever the threat, it was over, at least for the time being. That was good news but we were still scared shitless. And, it wouldn't be the only time. Over the next week or so, we would be called to GQ several more times, sometimes during the day and sometimes at night.

By late October, the crisis in Cuba and threat of war with Russia had been resolved. The Russians agreed to remove all missiles from Cuba and we agreed to remove our missiles from Turkey, which posed a threat to the Soviet Union. Shortly after this was announced, I found out that our planes had flown over four thousand sorties, meaning our aircraft were armed and in the air.

Without a doubt, the critical 'thirteen' days of this crisis was the closest the world came to an all out nuclear war.

SIXTEEN
MAN OVERBOARD

With the crisis over, our assignment was to remain off the coast of Cuba and monitor the removal of missiles agreed to by the Russians. The threat of war was over, at least in this part of the world, and it was back to our Cold War status. We continued to monitor the Russian's presence and launched aircraft daily to monitor the dismantling and removal of the missiles. Things were finally starting to calm down. We had no idea how much longer we would be here and Christmas was only a few weeks away.

We had been working twelve on and twelve off shifts, so after a good sleep we had time to relax. One day we were off duty so a couple of friends and I snuck our way along the catwalks to the bridge. There, we were able to climb the ladders up to the radar platforms. From there, we were able to watch the aircraft take off and land, supported by a hundred air dales on the flight deck doing their jobs. The screaming noise from the jet engines made things exciting. Every launch of an aircraft made me wonder if it was going to make it. Once released from the catapult, the planes would dip before rising with after-burners blasting to maximize speed.

Watching the planes land was just a thrilling. Each plane is coming in at over one hundred forty knots per hour, and has to line up perfectly with the rear of the ship. Then, it has to catch one of four cables with a tail hook to stop. If it misses, the plane has to full power up to lift off the angle deck for another try at landing. Only once in my two years at sea did I see a plane crash into the ocean trying to land. Unfortunately, the pilot was killed.

On this particular morning, the ship was doing about thirty knots into the wind to launch aircraft. During launch, two planes would often line up on the two forward cats at the same time. The flight deck crew would scurry around the aircraft to get them in the proper position for hook-up to the cats. We didn't see what had happened but all of a sudden the siren alarm sounded.

"Man overboard, man overboard," the boatswains mate yelled over the IMC. We didn't see what happened but apparently one of the jets, while getting into position for take off, made a turn catching one of the flight deck crew in his powerful exhaust wake. The crew member was blown over the portside of the deck and into the sea eighty feet below.

Instantly, with the alarms blaring, the Sara went into a full starboard turn. This is an automatic maneuver to distance the rear of the ship and props away from sailor in the water. The whole ship listed severely and we had to hold on tight. The destroyers along side and to our rear immediately slowed and performed the same maneuvers. This widened the ships into a circle pattern as a rescue helicopters were lifting off our flight deck. We remained silent in a state of shock.

The water was crystal clear and from our position, we could see the fallen sailor in the distance. We could see his bright yellow jersey which he wore to identify his job as part of the flight deck crew. As the ship continued to heel, we lost sight of him but could see the helicopter now far off, hovering over the water. The search went on for hours but the sailor was never recovered. Later that night, I remember seeing the message sent to Naval Command describing in detail, the incident along with his name, rank and serial number. It was the first time I witnessed a death at sea or any death for that matter. Unfortunately it wouldn't be my last.

SEVENTEEN
WELCOME HOME

We left Mayport for Cuba in mid October and arrived back in time for Christmas. Approaching our home port, we manned the rail in our dress blues. I had never seen so many family and friends anxiously awaiting our arrival. The Navy band was playing and people were cheering. It gave me chills like we had just returned from a war. Watching the greetings on the dock gave me a feeling of pride and a tear in my eye.

With the Cuban crisis behind us, most of the men went home for Christmas. I was not eligible for leave yet so a bunch of us stayed on board for Christmas. We went to the EM club most of the time, looking at the tree, and talking about home. Our friends with the cars were at home, so we stayed on base. New Years Eve was a headache for all of us after drinking too much of that 3.2 beer. This was our first Christmas away from home and some guys were upset. I really didn't care but it would have been nice to see Inez again. We were still writing but my sense was it wasn't as exciting as in the beginning.

The weeks went by and we were pretty much back to normal in port routines. Before we knew it, warm weather set in and we started driving to Daytona Beach. The beaches reminded me of where I grew up in New Jersey, except here you could drive your car right on the beach, and that was really cool. There were always a couple of friends over twenty one who had cars. We'd buy some beers and lay on the beach as often as possible. The girls were incredible and having a car on the beach sure came in handy. Lucky for us, we got to spend a fair amount of time there including spring break. I was surprised a lot of the college girls wanted to hang out with us instead of the college boys. I think it was our persona and maturity and the beer. We knew we had it better than the college boys. They had to go back to school; we had to go to the Mediterranean some time in March.

I didn't plan on going home on leave until after we got back from the Med. A couple of weeks before we were scheduled to depart, we were out at sea in preparation for the upcoming cruise. An emergency message was received that my father was rushed to the hospital and was listed in critical condition. My communications officer arranged for me to have emergency leave. I would have to fly from the ship back to the Naval Air Station in Jacksonville, where I would then board a navy flight to Floyd Bennett field in Brooklyn, New York. I was worried to death about Chas and thinking about my mom.

I packed a duffle bag and climbed aboard the COD plane; a twin engine prop used for mail and transport, and was strapped in tight for catapult launch. I watched nervously from my window what I used to watch from below the bridge- a plane being made ready for catapult launch. When I saw the Pilot salute, I knew it was off to the races so I held on tight. I felt my stomach go through my back then everything was okay, we were airborne. That was most unique and intense experience in my life.

I got a ride from Brooklyn to the train made it home in about eight hours. My mom was able to stay with Chas at the hospital. He had a burst appendix and could have died. Thank God he turned out okay. He and mom were home when I left to go back and I was relieved. The Navy takes good care of you in the case of an emergency.

EIGHTEEN
CROSSING THE ATLANTIC

It was near the end of March when we left Mayport to relieve our sister ship, the USS Forrestal CVA-59, and her task force, who had been on station in the Mediterranean for the past six months. We left Mayport with great memories of Daytona Beach, and me knowing that Chas was fine. It would take us roughly ten days to get there and we would not return until October, at least six months later. This was normal fleet duty rotation and takes place with the different Navy fleets around the world. Each fleet has at least one aircraft carrier as part of the main battle group. I was glad I wasn't on a submarine. They are deployed around the world too, but sometime they stay under water for up to six months at a time. I couldn't figure how they could have liberty because the Navy didn't want anyone to know where they were.

Our departure from Mayport was more emotional than when we returned from Cuba. This time there were even more families and friends hugging and kissing saying their goodbyes. After a while, the officers and enlisted men of the Saratoga began to board the ship and the band started playing 'Anchors Aweigh.' As the tugs maneuvered us away from the dock, people were waving and many tearful shouts of I love you. I felt really bad for all the kids waving bye to their dads. Everyone knew it would be a long time before they would see their loved ones again. Unfortunately for some, they wouldn't be coming back.

I had never seen the crew members so solemn. I was totally excited but sensed many people were sad knowing they wouldn't see their families or loved ones for at least six months. We were headed east into the Atlantic again but this time we would keep on our heading and cross about three thousand miles of open sea. The next land we would see would be Gibraltar, the gateway to the Mediterranean. Having endured the Cuban Missile Crisis, we weren't considered 'pollywogs' anymore. We were all one now, on the Sara, and this was the real Navy. We were in a cold war and issues between the United States and Russia were the same. It was democracy versus communism, freedom versus tyranny, and this was why we joined. It was a great feeling.

Crossing over it was flight ops as usual. We were lucky enough to be working eight hour shifts again so we had plenty of time to climb up the ladders outside of the bridge just below the radar. Everyone knew that exposure to radar waves could cook your balls so we heeded the warning signs. This area gave us the best view of the planes taking off and landing. We weren't supposed to be there and we never got caught. It was a great place to be day or night. Sometimes at night, the stars were so many and bright they overwhelmed you, especially if there was no moon. I never saw so many stars in my life, let alone the hundreds of shooting stars, we would see every night. It would be pitch dark and all you could hear was the water passing under fifty thousand tons of steel pushing through the water at twenty knots.

Along the way we ran into major storms. Some were so severe that the destroyer escort ships, who would normally ride along our port and starboard side, rode directly behind us to stay in our wake. The Sara, being so huge with four mammoth propellers, would smooth out the waves for hundreds of feet across and thousands of feet behind. Despite this tactic, the destroyers would pitch and roll so severely from left to right it looked like they might tip over. That's why the destroyers have the nickname 'greyhounds,' they just keep plugging through the waves; up and down, side to side. Meanwhile, the Sara would occasionally heave so violently from port to starboard, our typewriter carriages would move by themselves. And even though our bow was at least eighty feet above the water, waves of spray would come over the top. Now we knew what the old salts were talking about when they told us it would be so rough that they would have to strap us in to our chairs. I was lucky and didn't get sick but some of the guys did. After a day or two, it was beautiful again. That's how it was crossing three thousand miles of ocean; storms come and storms go.

A couple of times during our journey we needed to refuel. To do this, a fuel tanker would pull a hundred feet or so along our starboard side and maintain our same speed. Ships' company was stationed on a lowered aircraft elevator, and when in position, received a rope fired over by the fueling ship. Once secured, the fuel ship would attach and pulley a fueling hose over to the Sara. Once in place and secure, our ships' company band would play music for the entire duration. Refueling took quite a while so music was played to entertain the working crew. It was amusing to watch but you had to feel somewhat threatened should something go wrong. Accidents had in fact happened with other ships during refueling. When refueling was completed, the fuel tanker retrieved her hoses and slowly veered right, dropping behind our starboard side. With our tanks full of diesel and jet fuel, the band stopped playing and the Sara picked up speed. It can be somewhat tense watching two ships so close transporting fuel, but can you imagine the same maneuver to transport ammunition?

NINETEEN
MEDITERRANEAN SIXTH FLEET

It was early one morning when an announcement came over the IMC that land was in sight. Everyone off duty went topside to the flight deck. Gibraltar was to our left with its famous jagged shape. As we passed through the straights, we could see land far off to our right which was the coast Morocco and Africa. My body tingled thinking about my decision to join and realizing I was here, finally, realizing my dream of independence and adventure. I am eighteen years old and most of my friends are close in age. We are young, virile, fun-loving kids who are trained and prepared to defend our country at a moments notice. Our motto, 'live for today, tomorrow's not guaranteed,' so we are going to enjoy a sailor's life to the fullest; wine, women and song, and more wine!

After our long journey, we would stop at our first port of call, Naples, Italy, to take on supplies and give the crew some relaxation. Naples was the first of many seaports we would visit over the next six months as part of good will and 'R&R,' for the crew. The Saratoga would make port on multiple occasions in Greece; Italy; France, Malta, Spain and Turkey. I would get to visit places most people would never see in their lifetime.

The interval between visits normally was ten days to two weeks, making our deployment at least six months long. But, this was not the reason we were here, on vacation.

The primary purpose of the Sixth Fleet is to be ready for any possible military situation which may arise, primarily in the Mediterranean. Therefore, our readiness is first and foremost and can only be perfected at sea. All of our time at sea day and night, is spent conducting air operations, honing

the skills and performance of the pilots and support personnel. War games and tactical maneuvers are continually carried out with our task force to keep ship's company sharp,
whether it is the running of the ship in the engine rooms,
or monitoring sonar and radar systems in search of enemy
ships, subs or aircraft. Sea duty is intense but this is why we
are here. Visiting our ports of call is for international rela-
tions and rest and relaxation after being at sea.

For most of us Naples, the second largest city in Italy,
was our first time in a foreign country. As we approached
the harbor in the Gulf of Naples, the view was incredible. I
was looking at a beautiful landscape of Greek and Roman architecture buildings spread along a coastal cove of blue water with Mt. Vesuvius in the background. I never saw anything
like this in my life. This was definitely a different part of the
world compared to the US or the Caribbean. As we manned
the rail on our approach to our anchorage spot it was a different feeling from being home. We were now official representatives of the United States and the United States Navy,
the most powerful Navy in the world. We were expected to
be at our best at all times and damn it, we would try.

This was 1963 and back then, Naples was kind of like
Norfolk Virginia. It was the most visited port by ships and
sailors from the Sixth fleet year round and as a result, the lo-
cals were indifferent to our presence. As soon as we arrived
at fleet landing, kids swarmed around us trying to steal our
wallets, cigarettes, watches, all at the same time. We would
throw change as far as we could to get rid of them. The 'salts'
told us about these kids and to make sure we had change.

No one spoke English and we didn't understand Italian
or how many Italian liras equaled a dollar. They wanted our
dollars and they would try and charge a dollar for a beer
instead of three hundred lira, or about thirty cents. It took

a while for us to figure this out while being ripped off in the meantime. The bar girls really tried to take advantage knowing we were the new ship in port and tried to charge double for their drinks and services, Again we knew from the "salts" what we should be paying and quickly learned the art of negotiation. So we made the best of it over the next several days with liberty every other day. We toured the local ruins, took pictures and hit the bars, of which there were plenty. Some guys went to Pompeii but we decided to stay close to Naples knowing we would be back again during the cruise. We all agreed, being overseas in a real foreign country was exciting as hell but you needed to manage your money.

We left Naples and headed for open waters for more war games and air ops. This is what we do when not in port. It's all about readiness, and when we were done, the Sara headed north to Genoa Italy, a large port city located on the west coast of Northern Italy, close to Monaco, France and Switzerland. About half the size and population of Naples, Genoa is a beautiful city located on the Gulf of Genoa with the Apennine Mountains to the west. Surprisingly to me, it did not resemble Naples very much. I did not see the influence of Greek and Roman architecture.

What was really cool was the Saratoga was the first aircraft carrier to visit Genoa since World War II, some eighteen years earlier. Not even the 'salts' had been to Genoa, and as we came into the harbor, people were waving American flags and holding signs saying 'Welcome USS Saratoga." This was totally unexpected after our first stop in Naples. When the liberty launches pulled up to fleet landing people were cheering and hugging us. As we drifted from the dock, we followed our new friends to a local bar where everyone wanted to buy us a drink.

The Genoan's, especially the girls, were beautiful, many with blonde hair and blue eyes. Not that it really mattered but it was different after being in the southern part where everyone had brown hair and brown eyes. I figured it was because Genoa was up north, similar to our girls in the Minnesota, blonde and blue eyes.

Genoa was not a big city like Naples. It's more like a big town without all of the hustle and bustle. We were drinking wine for a hundred lira a glass, which was like eight cents; no one was trying to charge us a dollar like Naples. There were pretty girls around too, but it was like they were with their fathers or uncles, to the point where we didn't even suggest they might want to fool around. Later, our new friends invited us to the Carnival, so with wine in hand, we followed everyone from the bar to the fair grounds.

The carnival was an annual celebration of some kind. It had everything, Ferris wheel, bumper cars, just like ours back home. We were the only sailors there and everyone was friendly and speaking to us in Italian and broken English. We were drinking and flirting with the girls and having a great time. Time flies when you are having fun and with wine being so cheap, it didn't take long for me to lose my wallet. I had hooked up with some girl and we had been on the bumper cars, getting slammed. Sometime later when I realized my wallet was missing, I was in a panic telling my friends what happened when out of no where, a man and his daughter came to our table and he showed me my wallet. He saw my navy ID and found me in the crowd. I couldn't believe it and offered him money but he wouldn't take it.

"Grazie!" I said.

"God'a bless'a da US'a Navy," he said, giving me a hug.

Our first night in Genoa and we ended up staying at that Carnival to the end. Fortunately for me sailors look out for each other and one of our guys, an old salt First Class Petty officer, got me back to the ship without any trouble from the duty Officer. I could have been written up for a number of things. The next day I had duty but not until noon. Boy was that lucky considering my hangover. As I was getting dressed, I realized I didn't have my wallet. Oh, no, I thought I got it back? I started asking around and everyone I was with confirmed that the man with the girl gave it back to me. That was everyone except for Davis, the 1PO who brought me back.

"No man, when I woke you from the table you were upset because your wallet was lost, again. You were almost crying," he said. "We looked, but your wallet was gone."

Now I was sober and really upset. Losing your ID card is a very serious offence. Meanwhile, some of my other friends were just getting to go in town for the first time, so I told them about the Carnival and some bars we stopped at the day before.

I was a nervous wreck trying to think how I could have lost it a second time. Did some one steal it? My mind was working overtime trying to put pieces together. Finally I got off my shift compared notes with the guys again. We couldn't figure out what had happened. The next morning, my friend Smitty woke me up.

"Hey Spear, you are one lucky son of a bitch! Guess what I have?" Smitty said holding my wallet in his hand.

"You have got to be shitting me," I said, my heart beating. "How the hell did you find that?

"I didn't, some guy and his kid at that Carnival saw my Saratoga patch and showed me you're ID. Everything's there too, except for the five bucks I kept for me as a reward." he laughed.

I didn't know if he was kidding or not, I was still in shock that I got my wallet back at all, plus the most important thing, my ID card.

"Holy shit man, can you believe it? How awesome are these people? Thanks Smitty, I'll never forget this." I said very relieved.

I never expected to see my wallet again but I did, and that was a testimonial to how nice those people from Genoa Italy were. It also proved how nice my shipmates were too.

I found military friendship was different from anything I knew growing up. It wasn't like school friends or guys you would hang out with for the sake of hanging. Here, everyone depended on each other for something and no one held back. You were basically together 24/7. CR division was our home, where we lived and worked various shifts together. We all knew each other and socialized regardless of rank, except for CPO's and officers. We all got along with each other, but better with some than others and these turned into friendships. It was the same for all the divisions on the ship; you hung around with the people you lived and worked with. Smitty was one of my oldest friends who I first met back in Norfolk when I reported for duty. He was one of the six of us who shared the same sleeping area.

I left Genoa feeling really good about my new life. And even though we were heading out to sea again, it was never boring. I looked forward to my work and was always excited about the messages I received and sent. It was special to see privileged information, like our next port would be Valencia, Spain, followed by Barcelona and Majorca.

I realized as we approached the harbor in Valencia, that the coast of Spain was far different than Italy. There was a mountain range in the distance but nothing like Vesuvius outside of Naples or the Apennine Mountains west of Genoa. The architecture was noticeably different from Genoa and definitely different from Naples, reminding me more of Ponce, Puerto Rico which made sense since the Spanish discovered and settled Puerto Rico. There were even palm trees.

The city was spread out with the streets being narrow and the buildings no taller than three or four stories. Most of the action was centered near the harbor since Valencia was a very popular tourist city. The local culture was different as well. Spain was famous for bullfights, leather and wine. We couldn't find pasta or pizza but there was plenty of sea food and meat. We adjusted, drank the wine and found the bars. Again, we had another currency issue because Spain's money was pesetas, but like Genoa, we felt appreciated and the people went out of their way to make sure we got the correct exchange rate. I was beginning to like Spain the best. Our stay was only a few days as we would be heading north to Barcelona.

Barcelona was very beautiful and located at the northern top of Spain, close to the Pyrenees Mountain chain, which ran north and west to the French border. Barcelona was similar to Valencia, however, much larger and busier. And like every other city I had seen so far, older than any city in the States. I knew the US was almost two hundred years old, and I had seen pictures of our oldest cities, but none compared to Europe. I began to realize that so much of our history came from the places we were visiting.

Although we were young, we could see the cultural differences between Italy and Spain. On our first liberty, a bunch of us decided to see a bullfight. It turned out to be the worst thing any of us had ever seen and we left after the first bull was killed. While everyone was cheering, we were booing and being yelled at in Spanish by angry patrons. Later, we all agreed it was totally unfair to the bull, to have his neck cut to keep his head down, and then while bleeding and weak, be stabbed to death with a sword plunged deep into his chest. Where was the fight in that? Hell, this was savage even by our standards.

Another thing different was that Spain was more relaxed. Businesses would close at three in the afternoon and not reopen until six. They called this siesta time. The streets and restaurants wouldn't get busy before ten o'clock at night. Fortunately for us, that didn't apply to the bars. The girls were absolutely gorgeous too. Black hair and black eyes, just like the song: 'Spanish Eyes.'

The peseta was worth more than the lira and we got a lot for our money. Regardless, money goes quickly when you're having fun. I remember I had spent most of my money on this beautiful girl and I was sure she liked me. She started to get dressed and when I asked her to stay longer she looked into my eyes and smiling said something in Spanish. I looked at her puzzled. She came over to the bed and put her hand lovingly on my face. Very softy she said something in Spanish, which when translated, was:

"How can you speak of love when you have no pesetas?"

How true, how true was all I could think while getting dressed.

Our last port of call off the Spanish coast was the Island of Majorca, the largest island of Spain, located one hundred sixty four miles off the coast of Valencia. We anchored in the capital city port, Palma de Majorca, located in a protected gulf on the southern coast. It was getting warm by now so liberty included stopping at the beach. Majorca happened to be a very popular vacation spot for English and German nationals. For us, it was especially nice to be in a beautiful place, where most everyone spoke English. Contrary to Valencia or Barcelona, Palma reminded me more of Florida, in terms of the buildings and layout. There were Mountains off to the north and beautiful sandy beaches where we were. The beaches were covered with bikinis, and many without tops. This was truly heaven for a bunch of young sailors and a lot better than Daytona Beach.

The outside cafes were packed with tourists and of course, the US Navy. The first day in port, I met Emily, who was vacationing with her parents and their friends from London. She was sitting alone at a table for two and my friends dared me to sit down with her. I furthered the bet to five bucks if I got a date. I didn't see any evidence of another party, so with hat in hand, I asked if I could share the table. I looked over at my friends and smiled.

Emily had me immediately wrapped around her finger with her English accent, short hair, blue eyes and beautiful skin. She was drinking Compari and soda and I ordered a Cruz Campo beer. We hit it off really well and talked about London mostly. I was fascinated listening to her description of how she lived knowing not even the navy would get me to England. She told me how she had been to New York once which gave us something we could both talk about. When I described Asbury Park she compared it to Brighton, England, except their beach was stones, not sand.

I had never met anyone like her in my life. She was so very proper and I found myself trying not to fidget or say something stupid. When we left the café, we walked along the sea wall toward the hotel and beach where she was staying. She smiled a lot and said I was cheeky, what ever that meant, and I told her how beautiful she was, and I was serious. I explained to her how liberty worked and I wouldn't be off until the day after next. She made me promise to meet her at the café and I asked her not to meet another sailor in the meantime. She kissed my cheek, and I went looking for my friends, realizing that I had just met the most fantastic woman in my life.

My friends wouldn't pay me the extra five dollars for getting a date until she and I met up again. So I invited whoever was able to go on liberty with me to witness my meeting her. Sure enough, when we got to the café, she was sitting at the same table just like she said. My heart was thumping but I managed to introduce her to several of my friends before shoving them off. She laughed when I told her they were like wolves. I didn't say anything about the bet.

Including this day, I would have two more liberties before we left Palma. Emily and I spent as much time together as we could. We talked a lot about how we would see each other again. Hell, I only had about two years before I was out and I promised to do whatever I had too, to see her again. We were in love; I could tell. On our last day together, we promised each other that we would write every day. We hugged, kissed, cried and said goodbye, for now.

Back at sea, the guys who owed me the five dollars paid while calling me a lucky bastard, over and over. They all appreciated her beauty and poise and didn't understand why we didn't do it. They didn't get it; Emily was a refined lady from England, not a bar girl looking for lira or pesetas, although they had their purpose too. I realized meeting Emily had actually kept me out of the bars and saved me some money. Emily and I wrote to each other but it sure took a long time for me to receive her letters. Sending mail from the navy post office to the States is pretty fast, but trying to get a letter to England took a lot longer. The few letters I received overtime were sweet and kept me dreaming about seeing her again. It was nice to be in love.

We left Majorca and headed back to sea for a while before making our way up to France. Our first stop was Marseille, the oldest city in France and the second largest and was known as a cosmopolitan melting pot. When we arrived in 1963, Marseille was an unstable port city made up of Algerians, Russians, Armenians, Italians and Turks in addition to the French. It was more industrial than tourist looking and we were warned, before going on liberty, to stay in groups and not to straggle off alone. In addition to socialist and communist influences in this part of France, there were issues between the United States and Arab nations over Israel. And although we weren't that excited about liberty, after being at sea again, we were ready to let off some steam. As soon as we reached fleet landing, we noticed that the French gendarmes carried machine guns, an interesting contrast to the other cities we had been to so far. People weren't smiling at us or seeming friendly. After one day we would realize this was the worse port we would stop at.

One night on our way back to fleet landing, we saw a poster encouraging a vote for the Communist party. It had a big red hammer and sickle so we torn it down. All of a sudden, men started yelling and running toward us. We knew if we got caught we probably would have got our asses kicked, or been in a lot of trouble, so we ran like hell making it back safely to fleet landing. No one said shit until we were in our bunks and then we talked and realized how close we may have come to starting a major incident. Later, we decided that they were lucky that we didn't kick their asses, right then and there, and end this communist bullshit. We didn't bother going on liberty again, so it was good bye Marseille and good riddance to the Communist bastards.

Back at sea it was business as usual. Air ops, refueling and patrolling the Med. Deep down we were all wishing that something would happen to divert us from our normal routine; we were getting bored. Radio chatter was always present with messages involving rendezvous points or personnel issues, such as notifying someone that they have a new baby, or a family member was sick or died.

Just when we needed some excitement, the most incredible thing happened. A message came in that Seaman Smith's mother had passed away. The message was hand delivered to the Captain on the bridge. He in turn, gave it to the Boatswains Mate who was in charge of the announcements over the 1MC. On a carrier with close to five thousand men, it isn't easy to locate someone, especially with urgent news. It also isn't easy to have people perform their jobs right either.

The Boatswains Mate was instructed to locate Seaman Smith. The Boatswain, never having handled a request like this, grabbed the microphone, sounded his familiar 'boatswains' pipe' and announced over the the1MC public address system:

"Now hear this, Seaman Smith, your mother is dead."

Well, all hell broke loose. Seaman Smith, wherever he was, went nuts and had to be restrained and taken to sick bay. The Captain told the Boatswains Mate he would be courts marshaled if he did something like that again and explained that he needed to be tactful, and to never, ever announce over the 1MC that someone's mother was dead.

This has the ship cracking up for days.

Within a week another sailor's parent had died, this time, a Seaman Abernathy. The message was taken up to the bridge for the Captain but the same Boatswains Mate was on duty. Anxious to make up to the Captain, he took the message directly. Remembering what the Captain said last time, he reminded himself that he needed to be more tactful in finding Seaman Abernathy. He read the message, blew his boatswains' pipe and calmly announced over the IMC:

"Now hear this, all seamen whose last name begins with the letter a, fall out on the flight deck."

After seeing the men assembled he calmly announced:

"Attention, every one whose mother is still alive, take one step forward…..Not so fast Abernathy!"

Can you believe that?

Our new course took us from Marseille along the Cote D'Azur to the city of Cannes, France, the capital of the French Riviera. This was by far the most beautiful city, with giant palm trees along the Cote D'Azur, and a beach that went on for miles. We anchored just outside the harbor which was full of million dollar yachts. The water was blue, the sky was blue and the temperature was hot, so we strolled along the beach and gazed at the finest looking women in the world. The beach was unbelievable and better than Palma Majorca. Most women were topless and wearing the skimpiest bikini's we'd ever seen. This was the French way, we were told, total freedom of expression. We never saw anything like this back in the states, not even in Majorca or Daytona Beach.

We were having a good time but sailors didn't belong in Cannes. Cannes wasn't the kind of place where we could buy a bathing suit, change and go to the beach. This place was for the rich and famous, and 'wanna bee's,' and definitely out of our price range. The few girls we talked to were looking for rich husbands or a movie deals. After asking around, we were advised to catch a train to Nice, and to get off at Golfe Juan, about a half hour north. There we would find the Crazy Horse Bar, reputed to be the best bar in the entire Mediterranean. The train ran about every hour and traveled along the coast. It was really pretty and the trains were much nicer than our trains at home. We were there in about twenty minutes.

Stepping off the train we looked around, and there she was, The Crazy Horse Bar, a large two story building looking very American like from the outside. The American flag was hanging along side, but lower than, the French flag. In the main window, there was a neon sign with an Indian Chief riding a horse. Inside was a huge room, with a rectangular bar, and leather seated booths built around the perimeter. There were beautiful girls dancing around while the juke box was playing MoTown music. The place reminded me of a hotel with stairways going to the second level. Upstairs, there were private rooms like a hotel, for the ladies of pleasure who worked at the Crazy Horse. Downstairs at the bar, the girls came up to us in sexy broken English, happy to show off their mandatory health cards, something the French insisted on if you were to be a prostitute. That's right, prostitution was legal in France. We stayed as late as we could that day and caught the last train back to Cannes and fleet landing. We had the best time so far, dancing, singing and smooching with these lovely girls. When it was time for the Sara to leave, we left promising to be back. Please wait for us you lovely Mademoiselles. We'll be back! I never bothered with the beach at Cannes again. From all of us, a special Merci' to the guy who told us about the Crazy Horse Bar.

TWENTY
DISASTER AT SEA

Being at sea regularly becomes routine after a while, so we are unexpectedly drilled to achieve our highest level of performance. Ships actually compete for battle readiness and efficiency, with letters of accomplishment, e.g., 'E' for the winning ships, painted on their tower superstructure. It was now August of 1963 and we were out at sea in competition as a carrier group. I remember being on duty in the radio room the night of August 15 when around 0200 the alarms sounded:

'General quarters, general quarters, all hands man your battle stations.'

We had no idea what was going on. Because of our proximity to the portside catwalks, a couple of us ran out of the radio room and onto the catwalk. We couldn't believe our eyes. The entire back of the ship was on fire and deck hands were running around, many pushing wheel barrels loaded with bombs. We watched as explosion after explosion took place on the aft part of the ship. Things were out of control, and afraid of more explosions, we high tailed it back into Radio Central and secured the hatches. We didn't know what to do.

At 0800, our shift was over and we went back out to the catwalk. It was the worse thing I had ever seen. There were charred aircraft and some of them were being dumped overboard into the sea. There were scorch marks on the side of the five story bridge. Later, we were able to see the reports sent to the Naval Command Center, detailing the accident and its cause.

The report stated that at about 0200 hours, August 15 during night flight ops, an incoming aircraft on approach for landing was too low and failed a wave off warning, crashing into the stern. The resulting explosion and debris from the plane immediately spread to other planes parked on the flight deck, causing more explosions to aircraft and ordinance. The ship suffered superficial damage but fifteen planes were lost. The pilot and one other crewmember were killed along with nine flight deck crew members who were seriously injured. After what I saw, it was amazing many more people weren't killed. Unfortunately this type of accident would repeat itself, everywhere aircraft carriers were on duty, around the world performing air operations. For me and my mates, this would not be the only incident aboard the Saratoga.

TWENTY ONE
NAPLES REVISITED

As a result of the unexpected catastrophe, we returned to Naples for minor repairs and the off-loading of salvageable aircraft, which were not totally destroyed in the accident. Having been there earlier in the year, we avoided the local Naples scene and instead, took a couple of taxis to a winery outside of town. One of the older salts, a first class petty officer named Creel, had done this before and said it would be really cool. Hey, he was senior and had been here before, so why not?

We ended up in the country, and in a village where the locals didn't get to see sailors, especially American. It was all Italian and sign language; no English. Everyone was kind and doing their best to communicate and it kind of reminded me a little bit of Genoa. After some wine and beer Peroni at the local bistro, we were pointed in the right direction to the winery.

The village and the winery were hundreds of years old. We walked from the Bistro to a large stone barn located at the end of the village main road. Behind it, vineyards spread for as far as you could see. Creel, our old salt buddy, explained to the greeter that he had been there before, and that we wanted to do the wine tasting tour. The greeter, I'm sure seeing dollar signs, embraced Creel like a long lost customer. Not a problem, he responded in Italian, and handed each of us a small glass. We each gave him about two thousand lira or three dollars and started our tour, going from barrel to barrel, while hearing of the wine's virtues in Italian. No one understood what the hell he was saying, but who cared? We drank from every barrel and sometimes twice. We were the only guys there so he didn't seem to care either. Finally, he brought us over to the desert barrel. I don't remember if they made it or what, but there was a barrel full of Livorno, a yellow Italian liqueur which I remember from a drink called a Harvey Wallbanger. It was yellow and tasted like sweet licorice and it put us all over the top. Most of the guys were staggering as we said goodbye.

As we were leaving, the old greeter convinced us to buy an authentic goat skin flask. It was made from glass, shaped like a kidney and covered in rich goat skin. It had a leather shoulder strap and was worth the cost because it came with a fill up of our choice. I remember most of us filled up with the Livorno which was a big mistake. Livorno was a lot stronger than the wine.

We had a hard time walking back to the village and on the way, we were laughing and back-slapping to the point where we tripped and went down. Many of us broke our newly purchased flasks full of wine and yellow Livorno and our white uniforms were now stained purple and yellow. Oh shit! Nevertheless, we sat on the side of the road laughing.

We negotiated our way back to town and asked as best we could if someone could get us taxis. After much confusion, we realized there were no taxis in the Village. Fact was, they brought people in from Naples but didn't stick around. Oh boy, are we in trouble! Now we were getting worried. We started walking hoping for the best like maybe we could hitch a ride. Still stumbling and laughing at our physical condition and appearance, we managed to flag down an old open truck full of hay. A nice old man motioned for us to get in the back and understood Napoli, Napoli. Hell, our uniforms were shot anyway so we didn't particularly care about a little more dirt. It was sunset and we were comfortably spread about in the hay and sleeping it off, all the way back to Naples. Creel sat in the front seat with the old man and must have given him something. He drove us all the way to ship's landing and refused to take any money.

"Arrivederci," we yelled, waving goodbye.

We were really lucky to make it back in time for the liberty launch to the ship. Unfortunately, our luck wouldn't be so good when we requested permission to come aboard. The Officer of the Day had each of us put on report for our appearance which resulted in our restriction to the ship for one week; in other words, no liberty. Creel was more pissed off than anyone because he was a first class petty officer one level below chief, not low level seaman like we were, and a dirty uniform wasn't good for his record. Restriction was fine with us since the ship wouldn't need more than a week for repairs and we didn't care about going back into town anyway.

TWENTY TWO
THE ANCIENT WORLD

With all due respect, Italy is old but nothing is older than where we are going to next.

We left Naples and were underway for quite a while this time and heading to Athens, Greece. We passed through the narrow Straights of Messina, with Italy on our port side, and Sicily on our starboard side, separated by only three kilometers at their closest point. This was a sight to behold and nothing like I had ever seen, yet. I knew that people on both shore lines could see our huge warship and escorts.

Athens had us all excited knowing we were now going to see some of the oldest places on earth and different from anything we had seen so far As we approached our mooring spot, we saw hundreds of Greek citizens on the dock, waving American and Greek flags. Another great reception, I thought, like we had earlier in Genoa. This was going to be a good time. We anchored in the harbor of Piraeus, the seaport town of Athens.

Upon arrival in any foreign port, the crew receives a briefing on the culture and a reminder to all that we are representatives of the United States. A while back when we were in Marseilles, our briefing said to travel in groups of at least four, and to avoid a drink called Pastise because it contained a narcotic. In Athens, we were instructed to avoid local Greek liquor called Ouzo. They said it too could have a narcotic effect. Our conclusion we survived Pastise, we could survive Ouzo!

Piraeus was a large seaport town located several miles from Athens. It was a sailor's delight, with plenty of bars offering wine, woman, song; everything a young, single sailor away from home needs to relax. The Greek language was way different from the Italian, Spanish, and French we had been somewhat used to, and hardly anyone spoke English. So we reverted back to smiles, and hand jesters, which seemed to be the international way of communicating. As soon as we could, we wanted to try Ouzo, which was a Greek word, so it was easy for everyone to understand; Ouzo and a bottle of FIX beer please.

After we figured out Piraeus, we were anxious to get on with seeing Athens. I took my camera and looked forward to the ancient buildings. We hopped in a cab, and in about thirty minutes, we were in Athens. I had never seen a city built around the most ancient structures you could imagine. Naples had some old structures, but not as old as what we saw here.

We went everywhere with our cameras: the Acropolis, the Parthenon and posing in front of every monument and statue we saw. The structures were bright white in the sun, and the sky was always dark blue. Most of the ancient buildings were located on tops of hills with a view of the blue Mediterranean Sea. We toured over a couple of different days, but it was always special feeling to walk on ancient ground and touch history going back thousands of years.

One day in town, we met some Air Force guys who were stationed just outside Athens at a NATO airbase. They invited us to see their base and go to the EM club. They had a car so we rode with them into the countryside. After a quick tour of the base and a few drinks at the club, we went to their quarters. We couldn't believe how they lived compared to us. We lived in a compartment and slept in a bunk; these guys had a three bedroom house complete with some beautiful live-ins who served as their housemaids, servants, and whatever. After a night of fun they drove us back to Athens. For a while we questioned if we had all made a mistake by joining the Navy. Nah, we figured, as good as it looked, they were stuck there and we weren't.

TWENTY THREE
AN AIR SHOW DISASTER

The day before our official departure from Athens, we were host to the future King of Greece, Constantine, and his fiancé for an air show at sea. They arrived on the flight deck by helicopter as all off duty personnel manned the rail in dress uniform. Once they were onboard, and escorted to the Admirals flight bridge to observe the show, we were dismissed and weighed anchor. We cruised away from Athens escorted by a few ships, American and Greek.

After we launched a variety of different aircraft, ship's company was allowed to return to the open flight deck to observe the air show. A bunch of us were off duty so we posted ourselves up on deck just outside our radio room to enjoy the show. There were fly over's with squadrons in formation doing barrel-rolls and after-burner accelerations at very low altitudes. The show went on a while until the last two events were announced so everyone could pay attention and see what was going on. First, a Crusader jet would fly over dropping flares after which a Phantom jet would fire at them with air to air sidewinder heat seeking missiles. Sure enough, it went off perfect with each missile destroying their targets. Everyone was cheering and clapping.

The final event of the show was announced calling everyone's attention to the horizon in front of the ships' bow. The announcer on the bridge said to look for a dot approaching the ship just above the water traveling at mach two. This was a photo reconnaissance Crusader traveling at about fifteen hundred miles per hour.

"The photo Crusader will approach the ship about 300 feet above the water, and after taking his photos, accelerate straight up over the ship in a defensive maneuver," the announcer said.

Everyone stood scanning the horizon on the bow for the Crusader. By the time we saw the plane he was about three hundred feet in the air had popped numerous flashes and peeled straight upward disappearing into the clouds. There was a loud sonic boom and cheering as everyone started to leave the flight deck.

Then there were screams! Holy shit, Lookout! Then more screams. People were scrambling all over the place. As we looked up, we saw the Crusader falling, upside down, like a leaf, up, down, left, right and sideways. There was a deafening silence as everyone was frozen looking up at the sky. For a moment we could see the pilot in his orange flight suit and white helmet. It was taking seconds but it seemed like minutes and then, as if he got control of the plane, he nose dived into the sea about a hundred yards off the port side. No crash, explosion or sound. It was just like a knife going into the water and he was gone.

The moment turned into orderly chaos. Men ran to their posts, our ship and the ships around us immediately went into a sea rescue mode. For hours, the helicopters and escort ships searched for the pilot but to no avail. It was a tragic ending to what was meant to be a special time for everyone, our guests, ship's company and the proud brave pilots demonstrating their unique talents in flight. Later that night, the message to Naval Ops in Washington describing the incident blamed the crash on a flame out of the jet engine coupled with the pilot most likely suffering vertigo as a result of the falling, twisting motion of the plane.

The pilot was to be commended for his courage by steering the crippled aircraft away from the ship thus preventing further death or injury to personnel on the ship. This made us feel better for the pilot and in a strange way about the Navy as well. There was no blame to be placed here.

It was a solemn time at sea for the next ten days following our recent on board plane crash disaster, and the loss of a another pilot during an air show. Like me, most sailors never saw anything as catastrophic like this in their lives. Within a day of leaving Athens, flight ops, which were critical to our readiness, resumed as if nothing had happened. The ship and crew were back to a normal routine and we were now headed to Istanbul, Turkey. Even the old salts hadn't been there so this was going to be special.

TWENTY FOUR
DRINKING WITH THE ENEMY

We left the Mediterranean and Sea of Crete making our way through the Aegean Sea and the Sea of Marmara. We dropped anchor just outside Istanbul in the Bosporus Straight, which is the passageway to the Black Sea. The United States and NATO countries cruise the Mediterranean but the area around Turkey was open to the Russian Navy as well.

Istanbul is located on the Sea of Marmara and is where East meets West and Muslim and Christian cultures come together. As much as the skyline had the look of European and Mediterranean architecture, it clearly had a Muslim influence and was dominated with many beautiful Mosques.

As we prepared for liberty, ship's orders contained a reminder that we would likely run into Russian sailors who also frequent there. We were to be gentlemen and represent our country without incident or there would be serious consequences; in other words, no altercations.

Sure enough as we got settled in port we could clearly see several Russian navy ships. We had seen them almost a year earlier when we were on the Cuban blockade and they were easy to identify. Russian ships were painted with a much darker 'gray' than U.S. Navy ships, making them look almost black. Otherwise, their shapes were very similar to our destroyers and cruisers.

Liberty in Istanbul was by far the most interesting and exciting so far. Unlike Italy and Greece, we didn't feel compelled to go sightseeing. There were no ancient structures or ruins to see so we pretty much stayed in town. Our main focus was on the Bazaar and a place called the 'Compound' which we would see later, if we could find it.

The Bazaar area reminded me of an old movie with magic carpets and strange characters. It was full of narrow streets and tents with strange looking people huddled around oriental carpets drinking tea and smoking water pipes. Women wore veils and kids were trying to shine our shoes and beg for money. A bunch of little kids threatened to cut our shoes with their knives unless we bought a shine. We laughed while some older man came over and kicked them. We didn't see the stylish, trendy looking ladies we saw everywhere else.

It was difficult to find a bar let alone one that we felt comfortable in. There were no signs so when we asked where to go people would just point to a building. Usually, we had to go downstairs only to find a bunch of men wearing Fez's smoking and staring at us. After a while, we found a place we liked. It was well lit and in addition to tables, there was a stand up bar. More importantly, there were belly dancers.

Istanbul bars didn't have the usual prostitutes hanging around probably due to the Arab and Muslim influence in this part of the world. When we decided to take a table, one of the older Turkish men scolded us in broken English not to touch the girls. Alright, alright we said and after handing him a few bucks, we were seated and entertained by a beautiful belly dancer who had all of the trimmings.

Her hair was black, her eyes were black and her skin was cream. We had never seen anyone or anything like her. She clicked tiny metal cymbals between her fingers like castanets while spinning and gyrating her hips. We could hear some crazy music like a snake charmer would play while she danced. We were all mesmerized watching her slowly roll her stomach, sucking it in and out. She was barely covered in a see through sash and we could clearly see the outline of her breasts, hips and other areas of interest. Sir, can we get another round?

After paying for a few more dances we decided to belly up to the bar. Other sailors must have found out about the place because they started to come in. We noticed more belly dancers now performing at different tables. The noise level was getting higher but we could still hear the man yelling in his broken English:

"No touch the girls, No Touch!" So far so good we thought since no one started fighting or got thrown out yet for touching the girls.

Rather than look for other places to go we decided to stay where we were. The place was pretty full now. It was smoky and loud with crazy music playing in the background. We noticed some new sailors coming down the stairs heading our way toward the bar... There were a half dozen of them and they weren't American. Their uniforms were similar to our dress blues but different in color. Theirs was a lighter blue with white piping. Their hats were different too. They were wearing a light blue version of our flat hat with letters written in Russian.

We looked at them and they looked at us as they made their way to the opposite side of the bar. Except for the noise in the background, it was pretty quiet. For us this was a kind of holy shit moment, not knowing what to expect. We were in a cold war with these guys and Russia was the enemy. The possibility of war was still on our minds. While we had seen their ships from a distance, we never saw the sailors up close. This was a first for all of us from the USS Saratoga.

It ended up with them on one side of the bar and us on the other. We could hear them speaking Russian, a language completely different and unique from anything we ever heard. We couldn't help sharing glances and nodding heads trying to be friendly, but guarded, should we have to fight. I was praying no one in our group would say or do something stupid. Finally one of the Russians came around the bar to our side and said something. We all looked puzzled and had no idea what he was saying. Then, with a smile he hoisted his glass and with a heavy accent said "US Navy."

We looked at him and then at them. They all raised their glasses and without hesitation, we did as well. One of our Polish guys yelled "Nostrovia" which is like "cheers" or good luck. They yelled something back and we yelled again and then we started to mingle. Vodka started going down faster than a cheap pair of black sox! They couldn't speak English and we couldn't speak Russian but no one cared. We drank and laughed with our new Comrades while trying on each others' hats. It turned into a most special evening drinking with the enemy who were basically the same age as us.

Some time later that night, a bunch of sailors from the US and Russian Navy staggered out of that bar, hugging and yelling to each other, good luck and Nostrovia. Some of us, and I am sure some of them too, barfed on the way back to our ships. In remembering that night, it was too bad Kennedy and Khrushchev weren't there with us. The most important part of the cruise, and of course, no one had a camera to capture the diplomatic moment.

A couple of days later we had liberty again and with no restriction as to when we could go ashore. Most of ship's company had to wait until noon or 4pm, but not us we were on the mail boat going to shore at 9am. It was another beautiful day in Istanbul and it was nice to be walking around early in the morning.

We were told about this place called the 'compound' and knew that for us it was off limits. Since it was against the law to solicit prostitution in Turkey, the government sanctioned a 'red light' district called the compound. This was where women were confined in row apartments, and allowed to charge for their services, in order to pay off their debts. The area was a city block long with a guarded gate at each end.

There were a bunch of us so we needed two taxis. Being there early worked out to our favor for a couple of reasons. First, there wasn't any Navy shore patrol on duty to prevent us from going in. They wouldn't be there before 4pm when most of the sailors would be in town. Second, the ladies of the Compound were just getting up and were fresh for the new day.

As instructed by the taxi driver, we handed over five dollars each to the Turkish guards who nodded and smiled as we went through the double gates. The money was for them and had nothing to do with the girls. We smiled back and laughed taking our time walking down the street looking at the apartment windows. There were no cars, just apartments on both sides.

We looked left and we looked right smiling and waving while taking in the sights of young women sitting in their front windows smiling at us and waving desperately for us to come in. They were all scantily clad, some showing their breasts and some yawning. I think one was brushing her teeth while waving. We all agreed to do a walk by before making any selections.

No other country had a set up like this where there was such a line up of beauty. We joked about how we hoped they would have coffee and maybe breakfast for us since it was so early. After a while we made our selections and peeled off going our separate ways. Without going into details, it was the highlight of our Navy tour of the Mediterranean. Later back downtown in Istanbul, we compared experiences. No one got coffee or breakfast but we all agreed that Turkish girls were very clean shaven. So long Istanbul and thanks for the best and most interesting time so far.

TWENTY FIVE
HOMEWARD BOUND

We were near the end of our cruise and had one more port of call, Valetta, Malta. No one knew why we would stop there. It is a small island in the middle of the Mediterranean, between Sicily and Africa and was famous for where President Roosevelt, Stalin and Churchill met during the Second World War.

We only had one day of liberty there but I will say it turned out to be quite interesting. The city dates back before the Crusades and reminded us a little of what we saw in Spain. Unfortunately, there wasn't much for us to do meaning it wasn't as vibrant as the major cities we had been to.

What we didn't know was that there was an active Royal Navy base and boot camp for the British Navy's female sailors called 'Wrens.' The US had Waves and the UK had Wrens, how coincident was that? Lucky for us we ran into some friendly Wrens who showed us a pretty good time. What a coincidence that I would spend some time with Wrens like I did back at Radio school with the Waves. Valetta turned out to be a nice conclusion after all to our six months in the Mediterranean.

It was mid October now and we had been relieved and on our way home. There was a lot going on, especially with the air squadrons, who would leave for their bases prior to our arrival at Mayport. Time passed quickly going home. We were pretty relaxed without too much flight ops going on. The pilots and crew had done their share while on our deployment so I guess the Navy took that into consideration.

About a hundred miles from Mayport we began to launch aircraft. We sat outside again and watched as one squadron after another left the ship. After about an hour or so they were all gone and we could now see land. It wasn't long before we heard "all off duty personnel man the rail – full dress uniform." We needed to be dressed and man the rail in one hour.

As we slowly approached our berth, fire boats were shooting water high into the air while tug boats blew their horns. There were twice as many people waving and yelling on the pier compared to when we left. For many, this was the first time and longest they were ever separated from their loved ones.

It had to be a sad moment for those not on the dock to greet their loved ones. They were at home dealing with their grief. The reality was that during our six month deployment, ten of our shipments were killed as a result of accidents.

We lost five enlisted men, one ships company officer, and four pilots. It is hard to understand this kind of loss of life during peace time, but that is what can happen, especially on aircraft carriers.

TWENTY SIX
BLACK FRIDAY

After a short stay in Mayport, the air squadron personnel left and the Sara headed north. By early November, we were once again in the shipyard at the Norfolk navy base. After a long operation like we had, the ship had to go in for maintenance and repairs so she would be ready for our next deployment.

Several of us met here over a year earlier. None of us cared for Norfolk, especially in the fall. If it were summer, we would be hanging around Virginia Beach, but that wasn't appealing when it's cold and rainy. For a change, we spent a lot of our time on the ship and on base. Only the guys who lived close by would be going home for Thanksgiving and rest of us decided to save our leave for Christmas.

It was nice to be in dry dock again with out much going on. We had a large lounge next to our living quarters, and spent a lot of time in there watching television, which we could now watch live. We were anxious to catch up with what had been going on, especially the new music. As a result of being away so long, we were definitely out of touch.

Late one morning a bunch of us were in the lounge watching TV. I remember sitting with Corous, one of my Greek buddies, who convinced me to eat some anchovies and feta cheese which his mom had sent to him. Of course I tried them, but I was feeling nauseas and complaining how salty they were. All of a sudden, an emergency announcement came over the TV –

"President Kennedy has been shot, oh my God, the President has been shot!"

No one could believe it. As the stories kept coming in, we just sat there, crying, cussing and just staring in a daze.

We watched as Walter Cronkite cried announcing that our President was pronounced dead.

"Mother fuckers, who did this?" one of us was screaming.

I couldn't hold back my tears. Kennedy was my hero and a major reason I was here. I felt if it wasn't for him, I would have been a loser, probably in trouble or dead. He was my inspiration to do something positive in my life. That day in Casagrandes kept going through my mind:

"Ask not what your country can do for you; ask what you can do for your country," All of us felt sick and mourned all night long. We had lost our Commander in Chief and we were all thinking the same thing, what now? What's going to happen with the Russians? More important, just what kind of country did we come back to? How could something like this even happen in our country?

This was indeed the saddest day of my life.

TWENTY SEVEN
MAKING THE TURN

Repairs were completed and we made our way back to Mayport for Christmas. I had kept in touch with Inez and my mom and dad but I didn't let them know where I was or when I would be home. I wanted to surprise them as usual. I went home on a short leave and this time got to see most of the guys. Cal, Pete and McNeel were all home but much to my surprise, Pete and McNeel were married. I gave Pete the biggest hug first, then McNeel. They hit me with the news that Jimmy had died during the summer, apparently from an overdose of heroine. It was really sad, but I kind of had a feeling something could happen, after seeing him shoot up that night in the car. I asked Cal is he had seen Inez only to find out she had moved away. Hmmm, maybe her letter to me on this got lost or something?

It was great being together with everyone this time. We congratulated each other and talked of old times. McNeel told us about his ventures in the marines, which pretty much kept him in North and South Carolina, where he met his wife. He said he was going to re-enlist as he saw no reason to be up here around his drunken parents. Cal hated the Coast Guard and had six months to go. He didn't have any stories other than freezing his ass off while on patrol in the North Atlantic. They stayed up all night listening to my escapades. They were in awe of my stories and I couldn't stop talking. When we were done, I told them I was undecided as to whether I would stay in or not. I still had a little less than two years to go and I was a seasoned sailor now. I had not only served on the Cuban blockade, but also had completed a Mediterranean cruise as well. I was a 'Salt' now, and we drank to that. We got together for New Years Eve and

I missed Inez and admittedly was a little heart broken over her. Jimmy was another reason I found myself anxious to get back to my home.

After seeing Cal and my friends, I was looking forward to completing my tour. Although I loved the Navy so far, I never thought about making it a career, besides I had plenty of time to think about it. It felt good to be back with my ship-mates. Knowing we wouldn't go out to sea for some time, we started looking forward to the college girls at Daytona Beach. Another month or so and it would be hot again.

One day we were called to a company meeting in Radio Central. Our Commanding Officer explained to us that the USS Roosevelt, another carrier stationed at Mayport, was getting ready to leave for the Med, and that they were short Radiomen. They were looking for several volunteers. I'm not sure why, but my arm shot up instantly.

"I'll go," I said and that was that.

Three of us had volunteered and were accepted. We packed our sea bags and said goodbye to our friends. Hey, we'd still be neighbors and hang out until the Roosevelt left for the Med so that wasn't too bad. Lucky for us, she was parked directly behind the Saratoga.

TWENTY EIGHT
USS FRANKLIN D. ROOSEVELT, CVA-42

We walked up the gang plank to our new ship and showed our orders to the OOD, Officer of the Day. He got a good chuckle as did we over the fact we had just walked over from the Saratoga. The Quarter Master escorted us inside the hanger bay where we waited for someone from CR Division to come get us.

The Roosevelt, also known as the 'FDR' would be my new home for the remainder of my tour. She was basically the same design and layout as the Sara albeit a bit smaller and quite a bit older. We noticed this right away when we saw our sleeping quarters. Instead of the metal rack bunks we were used to on the Sara the FDR had the older hammock style rack. Oh well, such was life, and as long as we had adequate storage, no one cared. It was interesting meeting our new shipmates. Most were new to the ship, fresh out of radio school like me when I went to the Saratoga. To them my friends and I were the old salts now having been to Cuba and the Med. We had respect and our transfer was a very easy transition.

Within a week, we were underway for war games in the Caribbean, to prepare for the upcoming deployment to the Med. My friends and I from the Sara chuckled listening to our new friend's questions. We told them what to expect as we did our war games and readiness drills. After it was over, we pulled into Roosevelt Roads, again, for a break. For us, the place hadn't changed a bit from a year or so ago when we were there on the Sara, except this time there weren't any fights. I guess the Navy cracked down after that last brawl.

When with left Rosy roads, we thought we were going back to Mayport. Instead, we got a surprise. We would be stopping at our naval base in Guantanamo Bay, Cuba. No one we knew had ever been there, and although my friends and I had been around Cuba during the Blockade, we never came near our base.

Guantanamo Bay is located near the north east part of Cuba, far away from any cities, and at the opposite end of the island from Havana. No one was exactly sure what we did there but it was certainly different from any other port we had ever been too. It was huge compared to Roosevelt Roads. I think our stop there was just to let the base personnel see an aircraft carrier for a change, and mingle with the sea going sailors of the Navy. As things would turn out, that wasn't a very good idea.

Again we anchored out and took the liberty launch to fleet landing. Since we weren't allowed off base, we were allowed to wear our work uniforms. The base stretched out for miles surrounded by hills and vegetation and huge electrified barbed-wire fences around the base perimeter. We decided to go to the club first and buy some stuff later. When we got there, we noticed there were considerably more Marines than Sailors. Normally this would not be a problem, but the Marines are a different breed, all gung ho and all that shit. We knew from experience that they thought they were superior to us. Often to their surprise though, sailors could be tough as well. Usually Marines and Sailors don't drink well together. There was a contingent of marines on our ship, but they were clearly out numbered by sailors, so they kept to themselves. Their duty was to guard the Captain and Admiral, should he be aboard, as well as the nuclear weapons we carried.

The bar was huge inside the EM club and they were and drinks for twenty five cents. Cuba Libra, aka, rum and coke, and gin and tonics were flowing freely. It was crowded and you could feel the tension. Here we were just visiting for the day then sailing off to some other exotic place while the marines or 'jarheads' as we called them, were stuck on this base, hotter than hell and with no women. Where the hell did they go for liberty? You had to know they didn't like us being there, and our presence was pissing them off.

We stayed there long enough to get a good buzz and decided to go back to fleet landing and shop. We were outside a hamburger joint eating and drinking a beer when all hell broke loose. Jeeps, with Navy and Marine SP's, were racing to the club. We could see the club from where we were and the fighting had spilled to the outside. Last year there was a brawl between sailors at Rosy Roads, but nothing as big as this. This was Navy vs. Marines, and by far the biggest melee we had ever seen. All you could hear was yelling and the SP's blowing whistles and swinging clubs trying to get things under control. After a while, it was over and there were several naval ambulances on the scene.

Well that was that, liberty was cancelled and everyone was ordered back to fleet landing. While we were waiting to board the launch boats, the dock started to fill up with sailors, many of whom were bloodied, and some in handcuffs. It was a real mess and we were glad to get back to our ship. Well, we figured at least we got to set foot on Guantanamo, got a buzz and something to eat, and made it back with no trouble or bruises. Half the ship, including us, was on liberty that day. The other half of the ship was to go the next day, but we ended up leaving early the next morning. It was too bad they missed out on Guantanamo Bay, or was it?

It was great to finally be back in Mayport. Our deployment to the Med wasn't for another two months, so it was back to the beaches at Daytona. This time it would be with old friends from the Sara and new friends from the FDR. I spent as much time there with my friends as I could. Every day was beach blanket bingo and the most fun I ever had. The problem for me this time was that I would be the guy leaving while the boys from the Sara would get to stay. Oh well, the Med would be fun again for sure and the girls were a lot easier.

TWENTY NINE
SIXTH FLEET REDUX

The USS Franklin D. Roosevelt departed Mayport in late April 1964. We passed on the same stories about crossing the Atlantic and being tied to your chair in rough seas as we had once heard. Not this time though. After about ten days, we passed Gibraltar to rendezvous with, and relive, the USS Shangri-La. The three of us from the Sara were very lucky to be making a second Med cruise during a four years enlistment. Normally, a regular enlistment is boot camp, ship or shore duty, followed by ship or shore duty; typically only one sea duty assignment if any. When I volunteered for the Roosevelt, I knew that this would be a better way to finish my Navy career than sitting on base somewhere.

Deployment in the Med and being on station with the sixth fleet is pretty much the same routine, regardless of what ship you are on, or what year you are there. It is all about fleet readiness with air operations, war games and efficiency competition, followed by ports of call. I knew we would basically go to the same countries and ports as before. This cruise would be similar to our last except we would not be stopping at Marseilles, Genoa or Istanbul. I considered myself very lucky that I was able to see them last year. There would be two new places on our agenda; Taranto and Messina, Italy. Oh well, we would be in Cannes twice and the Crazy Horse Bar. What could be better than that?

Our ports of call would be more fun this time. Having been there before, we knew just where to go, for the least amount of money, and where to have the most fun. Our new FDR buddies really appreciated our knowledge and were happy to buy us drinks where ever we went. Surprisingly, we acted a lot more mature and restrained this time around, and we didn't spend as much money.

THIRTY
MORE DISASTERS AT SEA

Back on board the ship, our routine was the same as before. When we weren't working or sleeping, we would still climb up the bridge to watch flight ops. Unfortunately, just like on the Sara, we would witness more accidents. One I wouldn't ever forget because I knew the person killed.

We were watching planes taking off and that day they were launching one of a few heavy bombers. This plane was so big it carried a crew of three. Typical with other cat launches, the plane dipped a little below the bow. It happened so fast all we saw was a splash of waves come over the flight deck. Immediately, alarms went off followed by the ship turning; like when the guy fell overboard on the Sara. In an instant they were gone; pilots and crew. With so little time to react, the fifty thousand ton ship probably ran over the downed aircraft. Our ships searched for hours but to no avail. The plane and crew were lost.

A few days before this accident, I had an ingrown hair which had festered into a boil on the lower part of my neck. I went to sickbay and a young Doctor joked with me while giving me a cut and some stitches. He was a Lt. Commander and I could tell he was a flight surgeon by his insignia; gold navy aviator wings. These were worn by most of the senior officers on carriers. I was supposed to see him in a week to remove my stitches. A day after the crash, I read the message concerning the accident, and recognized his name and rank. He was one of the three pilots on board, probably getting in his mandatory flight time as an aviator. I was really upset knowing I had seen him die. Once again, this would not be the last tragedy I would witness.

On another occasion, we were watching a squadron of Sky Hawks flying in formation high up on the horizon behind the ship. We watched, as one by one they would peel off and dive to machine gun and drop a smoke bomb. The ship was towing a spar a few thousand feet behind and this was their target. After several passes, we happened to notice one plane was not pulling up as the others had done.

"Holy shit, holy shit," I remember saying.

The next thing we knew, the plane just slammed straight into the ocean, exploding on impact.

Jesus Christ, I thought, terrible things do happen on aircraft carriers.

THIRTY ONE
SHIP TO SHIP TRANSFER

By mid August, we had been to all of the same ports as last year. On one August night in Naples, six of us were enjoying an old favorite bar in town when all of a sudden, the Shore Patrol came in and told us to settle up, and get back to fleet landing. They waited while we got squared away and made sure we left. At fleet landing, there were other sailors, but no one from the FDR. It was no wonder, our ship had left. We looked out to where she was anchored and she wasn't there. What the hell was going on?

Earlier in the year, Greece and Turkey had threatened each other with war over the island of Cyprus. The island was occupied for centuries by people from both countries, but religion and other factors, had recently resulted in the death of citizens from both countries with totally different cultures. In addition, there were Americans living and working in Cyprus. There had been flare ups, but everything seemed to have quieted down except for now. While we were on liberty having our fun, the FDR and her task force was immediately dispatched to Cyprus for the possible protection and evacuation of American citizens.

One of the officers told us what had happened and explained that we were not in any trouble for missing the ship. We would spend the night on a cruiser which would catch up with our ship at sea the next day. We boarded the cruiser and were taken to available sleeping quarters. This was an older ship so we slept in the old navy style hammocks. We ate breakfast and shot the shit with their radiomen. One of them showed us the messages which were exchanged between the two ships and we read our names. It turned out we were going to be "high lined" to the FDR. What that meant was 'holy shit.' Similar to refueling, the cruiser would come along side the FDR and shoot ropes over to be secured. Then, one by one, they would 'pulley' us over the water in what's called 'the Pope's chair.' One look and it reminded me of an old electric chair with straps and pulley's attached to it. My problem was that if the rope broke, that chair couldn't float and that would be that. I would fall twenty feet into the water and get sucked under the ships.

The two ships came together at about thirty knots and about a hundred feet apart. I was never so scared in my life looking down at the water streaming by, while they were pulling me across a couple of feet at a time. After what seemed like hours, the six of us were all on board safely and the two ships parted ways. We sure had an exciting story to tell our shipmates and they couldn't wait to hear it.

The threat of war between Turkey and Greece was getting worse, and we ended up on station off of Cyprus for twenty one consecutive days. This was the longest I had ever been at sea with the exception of the Cuban Crisis, which the Roosevelt guys couldn't appreciate, because they weren't there. By the time we were able to leave the area, tensions were really high on our ship. So, the Captain, a very smart guy, announced that we would be having swim call. He knew this would calm everyone down. This never happened on the Sara and was a shock to all of us.

First, we launched several large motor boats, each with two Marines with guns. Their job was to patrol the area around the ship where we would be swimming. The water was eight thousand feet deep, but that didn't mean sharks couldn't be around. Second, they lowered the aircraft elevators to about twenty five feet above the water and attached cargo nets for us to climb down and up. Most of us just jumped, but not from the flight deck, that was too high.

We stayed long enough so everyone who wanted to got about a half hour to swim. It was a real hoot, and by the time it was over, everyone was pretty well relaxed. The marines didn't get to shoot any sharks or any sailors either.

THIRTY TWO
THE LIBERTY OF A LIFETIME

Cyprus finally calmed down and we were able to return to the final leg of our cruise. We headed immediately to Taranto, Italy, for much needed supplies, and then off to Messina, Italy, for a Fleet conference. We were getting close to the conclusion of our tour when the most incredible thing happened, perhaps in modern Navy history. The FDR lost one of her huge four screw propellers. Without it, the ship could not achieve and maintain enough speed to launch aircraft. Each prop weighs in excess of twenty tons and with the water being thousands of feet deep, there was no chance of recovery or repair at sea. Within a day our orders came into the radio room. We would stay on station near Gibraltar until the USS Independence CVA-62 could relieve us. She was en-route from the North Atlantic, where she was on duty as part of Fifth fleet. She arrived within a day or so and we headed back to the states.

Everyone assumed we would head to Norfolk for a new prop installation. Instead, our orders directed us to the Navy ship yard in Bayonne, New Jersey, just across the harbor from New York City. Apparently, Bayonne was the only dry dock available and large enough to accommodate a carrier. The entire ship was excited at the chance to see New York City. A few of us in CR division were from New York and New Jersey, but most of the guys were from other parts of the country. Except for this chance, they might never get to see New York City at all. For me, this was a chance to come home on my ship; another thing most sailors don't get to do.

The trip across the Atlantic took longer than usual but we finally saw that famous New York skyline on the horizon. As we got closer, we heard that familiar command:

"All off duty personnel man the rail, dress blues are the uniform of the day."

It was a beautiful, clear autumn day as we passed under the Verrazano Narrows Bridge. It was still under construction and would be the longest suspension bridge in the world, spanning the waters from Staten Island to Brooklyn. There was a huge American flag hanging from the bridge and the workers overhead were waving their hard hats and cheering. We looked up and waved back. Of course the unscheduled arrival, and unusual story of the USS Franklin D. Roosevelt, made the front page of the New York newspapers. Mayor Robert Wagner made a special welcome for our arrival to the greatest city in the World. As it turned out, we would be there for fourteen days and being in dry dock, only a skeleton crew was required to stay on board. This was a unique chance for me to show my friends the sights and sounds of where I was from.

Once we were in dry-dock, we left the ship and walked to a local bar called 'Feeny and Addies.' This would be home base for us since we knew we couldn't afford to go to New York more than a couple of times. As a small city and navy ship yard, Bayonne had been dead since the Korean War ten years earlier. According to the locals, we were the first carrier to ever be in dry dock there. I figured the FDR would probably employ people with double and triple overtime just in time for Christmas.

As soon as we could, we made our way across the harbor to New York City. I had been there a couple of times and knew a little bit more than my friends. The guys were so excited we actually went to the top of the Empire State Building. We were the only sailors in uniform and everyone was especially nice to us. The drinking age was eighteen so we hit all the joints, especially around Times Square. The guys couldn't believe their eyes with the nude shows and theatres. After Chicago, Norfolk and Mayport, nothing could compare to Times Square. I had to keep our country boys under close supervision though. There was a lot of wine, women and song going on and they were getting dizzy from the neon lights. I had never seen so many guys buy post cards in my life.

Back at the ship we planned a trip to the Jersey shore. I called Chas to see if he had got me a car yet, or if I could borrow his for a day or two. I had been sending him money to help out and a portion of the money was to be used to by me a car. Lucky for me he was home.

"Sure, no problem" he said. "Where the hell are you bubby?"

I told him briefly what had happened and that we were in Bayonne. He said come on home, the car's ready. He sounded excited and so was I. Chas came through and actually got me a car. Great!

There were four of us, including me, so we grabbed the North Jersey Coast train at Newark. They enjoyed the ride to Belmar, even though there was no bar car, and we didn't have time to get a beer. It was a ten minute cab ride to the trailer where I told them my retired parents lived. I couldn't think of one reason to let them know I lived in a trailer. My car wasn't visible until I looked around the back side of the trailer.

I couldn't believe my eyes. I wanted to scream while we stood there looking with no one saying a word. My friends were polite enough not to laugh. Here it is 1964, I am twenty years old, and I am staring at a 1955, black, four door Cadillac Sedan de Ville that Chas picked for me? Don't get me wrong, it was a beauty and perfectly suitable for a gangster, limo

174 **NAVY DAYS**

driver or funeral director, but not a twenty year old. Couldn't it have been something a little sporty?

Just then Chas came around the corner, beaming with pride. He had that same damn look when I was sixteen and he told us that he bought a 'mobile home.' He gave me a big hug and anxiously, starting introducing himself to everyone. I watched their faces as he tried to shake their hands off and had to keep from laughing at their expressions. When he was done, he pointed to his car, looked at me and said,

"Well, what do you think bubby? Ain't she a beauty?"

"Bet your ass she is," I said. "You did good dad." I didn't want to hurt his feelings knowing that he bought this car for himself. He always wanted a Cadillac and I knew not to ask where his car was, he didn't have one. This was it. I left Chas yakking it up with my friends while I went inside to see my mom. She was sitting watching the television. She did a double take when she saw me, then smiled. I hugged her and gave her a big kiss. She really didn't mind when I said I had to go but would be back soon.

Well, at least we had transportation. See you in a couple days dad, and off we went. As soon as we left, I told them my dad was an old mob guy. We all laughed. Anyway, there we were, four sailors in uniform, riding in a Cadillac Sedan de Ville. We rode in style and comfort. We had power steering, power windows, power seats, air conditioning an automatic scanning am/fm radio and an automatic head light dimmer. Can you believe all of that in a 1955 car? Although summer was over, we drove around the beach areas along Belmar, Asbury Park and Long Branch, stopping for some hot dogs, clams and beer, before heading for the Jersey Turnpike to New York City.

We drove through the Lincoln tunnel and were in the city by late afternoon. The windows were down and the

radio was blasting Martha and the Vandellas. They were singing 'Dancing in the Street.' Every time we stopped at a light,
people would look at us, waving their approval and some
would even sway to the music. We tried our best to get girls
to come in the car with us but that didn't work. I don't know
how I parked, or even drove around with a car this size,
without having an accident, but I did. Everything was cool.
We hit a few bars and decided to go to Long Island. One of
our guys lived about thirty minutes away in Manhasset, so
we spent the night and part of the next day there before
heading back. His parents were really nice and we slept well.
I dropped the boys off back at the ship and drove the car
back home. Our time in Bayonne went by fast but what a
treat it was to have my friends in that big old Cadillac, tool-
ing around New York City.

Thanks for the car Chas, tell you what, you keep it!!

THIRTY THREE
NOT SO FAST FDR

Although we were in New York and already on the east coast, we had to go back to the Med and finish our duty assignment. This came as a surprise to everyone considering the time and distance to go back just for a few more weeks. We had our new prop and were fit for duty, so we crossed the Atlantic and went through the straights of Gibraltar again to relieve the USS Independence. This was accomplished on October 29, and we resumed our deployment schedule. We had three more ports of call between air operations: Cannes, Palermo and Valencia.

On November 2, we arrived in Cannes for what would be my last time. We had been here earlier this cruise, and once again, I rounded up the guys for the train to Golfe Juan and the Crazy Horse Bar. My friends and I from the Sara knew we would never see this place again, and had the best time ever. It was funny how the bar girls remembered us in particular.

Our next stop was Palermo, Sicily. It was early December and it was cold. Palermo was kind of like Naples but not really. It was much smaller and had more mountains around the city. In fact the city was very hilly. The people had a more serious way about them. A lot of people wore black clothes and were mostly older. I think they hid the girls because we didn't see the kind of bars we saw every where else. After seeing the Godfather movie years later, it was easy for me to remember Palermo. I think if it wasn't so cold, we might have done more sight seeing, but it was easier to just sit around and drink that delicious Moretti beer, and talk about what we were going to do when we got home.

Finally, we dropped anchor in Valencia, Spain. This was a time to really celebrate since for many of us, this would be our final 'Med' cruise ever. I remember it was so cold we had to wear our pea-coats, which got me in trouble later that night. Anyway, the good thing having been here so many times before, we knew right where to go, and where the best girls were. We intentionally came out to party and celebrate our final departure from a part of the world that would forever last in our memories. The wine, beer, music, dances and kisses went on all night until it was time to leave. Most of us were pretty drunk but we stuck together and took care of each other getting safely back to the ship. My problem with my pea-coat happened along the way.

We decided to sneak some booze onto the ship for the long journey home. I decided on a bottle of rum, and stuck it inside my pea coat sleeve, pointing downward from my arm pit. I just had to remember not to hang my arm straight down. A couple of the other guys did the same thing. None of us had ever done this before, but we figured what the hell, this was our last cruise and a special celebration. Everything was fine climbing up the gang plank until I saluted the OOD.

"Request permission to come aboard, sir," I said rendering and holding my salute.

"Permission granted," he replied returning my salute.

I dropped my right hand and the bottle of rum slid down my arm, smashing on the deck.

"Quarter Master, put this man on report," said the OOD.

"Yes sir. Sailor, come with me."

Well, there you go the one and only time I ever tried something like that and I got caught. I had to go to Captains Mast and my punishment was two weeks restriction to the ship when we returned to Mayport. Even though this would prevent me from going home for Christmas, my punishment could have been much worse for trying to bring alcohol on board the ship. I got a break because the Captain knew I was pretty seasoned and getting out in a few months.

A few days later, we were relieved by my former ship, the USS Saratoga. Each radioman has his own signature or ID so I was able to send messages back to the guys I knew on duty with the Sara. It was pretty cool telling them about the Crazy Horse again. Wow, I thought, how ironic was that?

We headed west passing Gibraltar and into the Atlantic. We were homeward bound at last. Originally we should have been back in October; now it was December. Our duties were pretty much the same as coming back on the Sara. Once again all aircraft were launched prior to our arrival, and we 'manned' the rail to another major welcome home celebration. We should have been back in October but the Cyprus War and losing a prop, made this cruise longer than normal. It was December 22nd and we were back just in time for Christmas. The crowds on the dock were waving and cheering and once again I thought about those who didn't return with us.

Just like my last cruise on the Saratoga the year before, we lost several Pilots and Seamen on the USS Franklin D. Roosevelt Mediterranean cruise of 1964.

THIRTY FOUR
MOM HAD A BABY

My two week restriction to the ship prevented me going home for Christmas, so I was in our lounge when I watched the ball drop on New Years Eve, 1965. This was definitely my year. I was going on twenty one, I would be getting out in May and I had just made third class petty officer, not bad for a high school drop-out. I was finally on my way home for a short leave and I was feeling on top of the world. I was a short timer!

Cal, Billy and Bruce were all out of the Coast Guard now and were at home. I went straight to Cal's house to settle in. I'd catch up with mom and dad later. That night we all got together for a mini reunion at Casagrandes. I couldn't believe Lou and Diane were still there, let alone still married. The place had changed a little, and there were younger faces hanging around, but over all, it was the same. The juke box and pin ball machines were still in the corner. It had been a long time since we all stood there together and it felt good. We walked next door to Kroh's bar and laughed listening to each other's stories until the place closed.

After a day or so, Cal and I went to check in with Chas. Holy shit, I thought, would my life ever be normal? Once again, Chas had an unexpected surprise for me.

My tiny little bedroom was now a music room. Where my bed used to be, there was now a baby Hammond organ.

"Come on Edna, play something," he said to my mom.

Mom pulled out the bench, sat down and started playing what sounded like 'Frankenstein' music. Chas was grinning like a 'Cheshire cat.'

"So, what do you think of 'baby'? Your mom really loves her and I'm learning to play too," he said. I noticed the keys had numbers on them.

Baby I was thinking, and then I remembered. Near the end of our cruise, one of his letters said something about a surprise and that my mother was going to have a baby. I remembered telling the guys about it who came to my house when we were in Bayonne, especially after the Cadillac deal. I joked he was flipping out, but now I understood; the baby was the organ. It was something my mom always spoke about so he bought one for her. Now, the trailer was a one bedroom with no room for me. Good, I thought, now I was really out. Cal and I gathered the rest of my clothes and took them to his house. At one point we had to stop the car we were laughing so hard.

Cal wasn't anxious to get to work so we just hung out. It was just like old times, no agenda, having some beers and chasing women. While I was home on leave with Cal, I didn't need a car. I would, however, need to drive back to Mayport so I could bring my stuff back when I got discharged. We stopped to see Chas so I could remind him I would need 'my' car to drive back. He twitched a little and looked away.

"Alright bubby," he said turning around. "Let's go to Bernie's."

"Okay, let's go," I said.

I didn't see any need to remind him that I already had a car, a 1955 Cadillac.

Chas jumped into Cal's car and we headed off to Bernie's body shop. I remembered Bernie from when I was a little kid. He would scare the hell out of me and I cried whenever he came over our house. Bernie had two full sets of teeth on the top of his mouth; one complete set behind the other and one day Chas made him show me. I never saw anything like that again.

Anyway, Bernie had just repaired and painted a wrecked 1956 Cadillac Eldorado convertible which he would sell me for $300 on a time plan. I gave him $25 down and he promised to have it ready and sparkling by the time I had to leave. I thanked him shaking his hand and trying not to look at his teeth. Originally it was red with red leather interior and a black top. Now it was white to hide the body work. I didn't care, it looked sporty and I was a Cadillac man now. I think Chas was jealous as hell. Cal was cracking up the whole time.

THIRTY FIVE
BACK TO REALITY

It was time to get going so I said good bye to everyone and hit the road. The drive from Belmar to Jacksonville was nuts. The only modern road was the Jersey turnpike then the Chesapeake Ferry Boat, and route 17 and 301 and finally US 1. There was no I-95 like we know it. All in all it took about thirty hours. I was so excited to get back I drove the whole trip only stopping for gas and to pee. I made it all the way into downtown Jacksonville before dozing off and tapping a guy's bumper who was stopped at a light in front of me. He did me a big favor and let me go, probably because I was in uniform. It was a good thing too, because since joining the Navy, I never bothered to get my drivers license. I only had an expired learners permit from New Jersey.

My buddies were really impressed with my car, especially the guys who rode in the '55 mob car. The '56 Eldorado was a sporty two door coupe and was the most expensive Cadillac made. It had every gadget you could imagine and magnesium wheels. They couldn't believe I only paid $300 for it, but that's what Bernie got for scaring me. Even though it was still chilly, we would put the top down and cruise around. We had one more Caribbean cruise coming up and then it would be warm in Mayport and we'd be ready for Daytona Beach.

This deployment would take us back to Rosy Roads again for war games and the same old drills, air ops, general quarters and overall combat readiness inspections. Fortunately, we wouldn't have to go ashore at Rosy Roads again. This time it would be somewhere new, St. Thomas, Virgin Islands. None of us had been here so we were excited to be somewhere in the Caribbean other than Puerto Rico.

St. Thomas was more beautiful than any of the other ports we ever visited in the Caribbean including Ponce and Guantanamo Bay. The culture wasn't influenced by the Spanish as was Puerto Rico. St. Thomas had its own Island culture which was related back to African slaves who settled there. The crystal clear water, white sandy beaches and tall swaying coconut trees swept you away. The town was relatively small and surrounded by high hills with stately homes. Not far across its harbor, you could see the island of St. John. This was the tropics and was unlike anyplace I had seen before, including in the Med.

Unfortunately all men are not created equal including sailors. Quite a few of our guys back then were prejudice against blacks. Hell, the civil rights movement was still going on back at home. You wouldn't hear it on the ship, but you knew it was there. Looking back though, I must say that on both ships, I never saw a black/white altercation. Call it the 'Military Code of Justice.'

The people of St. Thomas are their own people, mostly black and with their own native culture. Their country is a possession of the United States, and I don't know what all that means, but I got the feeling they really didn't care much for us being there. We enjoyed going to hotel beaches and pools and the local drinks. Downtown in the large bazaar shopping area, there were local arts and crafts, paintings, drifters, and quaint bars and restaurants tucked away in small alleys.

One morning I was notified I had been assigned Shore Patrol duty that day. I had never done this before but now I was a Third Class Petty Officer and anyone my rank or above, could be randomly picked. I was outfitted with my SP arm band, guard belt with night stick, hand cuffs and whistle. Training was on-the-job and fortunately I was paired up with a First Class Petty Officer who knew the ropes. We were as-signed patrol in an area inside the bazaar. I was thinking how cool and sharp I must look, damn, no camera.

It was late afternoon and it was hot. The area was quite busy with our task force of ships being in town along with the tourists. My partner and I just walked around smiling, saying hello and talking to girls once in a while. As the day went on, we got relieved for an hour or so to get some-thing to eat. So after having a few cold ones and relaxing for a while, we assumed our patrol. The sun was starting to set behind the western hills and it was starting to get dark. The lights in the bazaar were lit up like a festival and the alley lamps started to light. We noticed there were more lo-cals out on the street than earlier. It was disturbing that the younger boys, in particular, would sneer and mutter as they past us by, but our role was to nod and smile.

Wouldn't you know that just about the time we thought everything was cool a tourist couple ran up to tell us some of our guys were being beat up in an ally. We took off running in the direction to where they pointed, and sure enough as we rounded a corner, there were four sailors drunk, bloodied and swinging away at about eight locals. For every punch our guys landed, they got hit with two or three times as many. We drew our nightsticks and started blowing our whistles to get their attention. We started pulling our guys away and pushing the locals out of the way with our sticks. After we had them separated, I made the mistake of facing one of my guys with my back turned, 'BOP!'

I took a punch to the back of my head which hurt like hell and knocked my hat to the ground. All I could see was the dirt on my white hat. Shit! In a self defensive move, I spun around with my night stick and whacked a couple lo-cals across their faces. They took off running and I picked up my dirty hat. My partner had all four sailors jacked up against a wall and asking for my handcuffs, handcuffed the remaining two guys to each other.

We stuck their hats on them as best we could and escorted the poor bloodied bastards back to fleet landing. I was pissed off and my head hurt. To make things worse, while we were standing holding onto these guys waiting for the liberty launch, the guy next to me started to piss on my leg. Somehow with his free hand he was able to do this. My partner started laughing and so did I. After all, I couldn't beat up a guy in cuffs. So I shoved him and the guy he was handcuffed and both went tumbling to the ground.

Despite being mad, I felt sorry that they would have to go to Captain's Mast for punishment. I'd been there once before and it wasn't fun. The good news was I didn't ever have to worry about Shore Patrol duty again. Suffice it to say, St Thomas was nice and I did get to spend another day on the beach, but that was my last port of call, and my last time at sea for the next thirty six years.

THIRTY SIX
THE FINAL DAYS

When we returned to Mayport and the ship was not scheduled to leave again until after my official discharge date of May 28, 1965. There wasn't anything to do except work and have fun on our days off. It was warm now and we'd put the top down on that old Cadillac Eldorado and head for Daytona Beach as often as we could. I did my best to avoid any trouble being 'short,' but as it turned out, it wasn't always easy.

We still had our duties in the radio room and one night we were on the Midnight shift. About 3am a few of us decided to go to the mess hall for breakfast. We yelled into our duty officer that we were leaving to get some chow. As we headed out, an Ensign, the lowest of officers, yelled out, "Don't forget my sweet roll."

For anyone else, this would not have been a problem. In fact, we would bring stuff back anyway, but not for this guy. He was a dick and was always intimidating us enlisted men for cigarettes, cookies, you name it. It was like officer harassment.

"Sure, no problem sir," I said leaving the room.

After we finished eating, I took and unwound a sweet roll to about eight inches long, sprinkled it with red pepper, pepper and Tabasco sauce. Then, I smeared it with jelly and carefully rolled in back into a bun. The guys were amazed and cracking up. I had to be careful putting it back together I was laughing so hard.

When we got back to the main radio room, he was in a side room. I set the roll on an empty desk away from our stations and we sat there with our ear phones on doing our jobs. Every time we looked at each other, we almost burst out laughing in anticipation.

He didn't know that we had come back but finally the 'mouse' came out of his hole. Out of the corner of my eye I saw him walk over to the far desk and pick up the roll.

"Ah, ha, what do we have here?" he said. "Is this mine?"

"That's not yours, sir. That must be someone else's because they were all out when we were down there." I said. The silence was deafening.

"Well, you guys know the rules, finders' keepers, losers' weepers" he said. Yeah, I thought, just like he did with the cigarettes

We looked at each other waiting to burst. Sure enough, in about two minutes we heard him yelling and running for water. He came back pissed off and wanted to know who did this. We were all talking at the same time; we didn't know what he was talking about. I politely reminded him that there were no sweet rolls when we were there. He kept glaring and wiping his mouth with his handkerchief.

"You all will be punished," he said. "I am putting you all on report and you will never disrespect a naval officer again."

As a ranking third class petty officer and shift supervisor that night, I made it a point to tell the relieving duty officer what had happened, and that we didn't know anything about that sweet roll. I also reminded him that we always bring something back for 'you' guys. We figured the Ensign would be too embarrassed to tell anyone how he'd just grab a bun without even knowing where it came from. We laughed hard that night for a long time, but I was worried that someone was going to brag me out and I would get busted. Nothing ever happened though, and that Ensign never bothered any of us again.

The worst thing happened the weekend before I was getting discharged.

Miller was another good friend of mine, and he and I met a couple of girls who invited us to a house party. We ended up at an apartment full of girls and guys, many of whom were from the base. The music was blasting, people were dancing and the drinks were flowing. It was a great party and I was just getting into it with this girl when the apartment door was kicked open. A bunch of cops came into the apartment and rounded us up for an ID check. It was the local Jacksonville Beach police who weren't fond of sailors and enjoyed any opportunity to break balls. They unnecessarily kicked the door in like this was a drug bust, which it wasn't, believe me. This never happened where I came from, but in Florida the drinking age was twenty one, and they had the 'right' to enforce it, even if you were on private property. The police checked everyone's ID; if you were under twenty one, it was off to jail.

It was late May and although I would be twenty one in a matter of days it didn't matter to the police. Miller was nineteen and we were both screwed. In addition to being in trouble with the law, the police would turn us over to the shore patrol who would turn us over to the naval authorities. Before the shore patrol arrived, we were charged with underage drinking and disturbing the peace; we were to appear in court about three weeks later. We weren't a priority pick up by the navy, so after a night in jail, we were released to the shore patrol and rode in the back of a Paddy wagon to the ship. We talked for a while but then I started feeling sick, wondering how this was going to affect my discharge which was three days away. As we were escorted onto the ship, the shore patrol handed papers to the OOD, who told the Master at Arms to write us up. We would be notified when we would appear before Captains Mast for punishment. Shit, this was going to mess up my discharge for sure.

I couldn't sleep that night and was now worried about my car. Fortunately, the next day I got one of the guys who went home with me back at Bayonne, to bring it back. I had to pay his cab fare and promised to give him all my phone numbers for the local girls. I was praying the car was still where I parked it and it was. He brought it back safely with no problem. That was a blessing.

I was beside myself with this Captain Mast hanging over my head. All I could think of was that my discharge would be delayed until I appeared in civil court and depending on the outcome of that, I could end up with a less than honorable discharge. There was no one to talk with for advice on my issue and I couldn't sleep. I couldn't believe after all that I accomplished, that I'd get screwed in the end. I was angry God Damn It! Give me one valid reason why any person old enough and willing to die for our country has to be twenty one years old to drink? Kiss my ass if you disagree.

THIRTY SEVEN
MY MIRACLE

I was up extra early on the morning of May 28, 1965. I hadn't been notified of any change to my requirement to be at Personnel at 0900 for military separation. I was nervous and showed up with about ten other guys. When it was my turn to be interviewed, I kept waiting for the shoe to drop but it didn't. The Personnel CPO went over various offers for me to re-enlist, one of which was a three thousand dollar bonus and guaranteed shore duty in either London or Rhoda, Spain. A quick thought of Emily, the girl I met in Majorca from London ran through my mind, but then I remembered she stopped writing a long time ago. I also thought about a job my dad assured me was waiting for me. Chief said the offer was good for ninety days as he handed me a folder with papers for me to sign. In the folder was my DD-214 with my Honorable Discharge papers and my final Navy pay. I was honorably discharged and would now have to serve in the Naval Reserve for two more years. We shook hands and that was that. No mention of Captains Mast. He wished me good luck and said I was free to leave the ship anytime. I was now a civilian and a member of the Navy reserve.

I thought I was going to piss my pants as I literally ran back to CR division. I needed to pack up and get the hell off the ship as quickly as possible. The guys were anxiously waiting to find out what happened. I gave them all the details as they stood there shaking their heads and patting me on the back.

"All right, who wants what?" I said, throwing stuff on my bunk that I wouldn't be taking home with me. Kelly got my phone book as promised for getting my car. I stopped by the radio room and said goodbye to the guys on duty including the officers, shaking hands with each of them, especially the Ensign I lit up that night with the sweet roll.

Walking through the passageways, I started feeling emotional; kind of sad and glad at the same time. When I got to the gang plank, I handed the OOD my papers, saluted him and said,

"Request permission to leave the ship, Sir."

"Permission granted," he replied returning my salute.

I turned, saluted the American Flag, and with my sea bag over my shoulder proceeded down the gang plank to the dock. On the dock, I looked back at the huge aircraft carrier, USS Franklin D. Roosevelt, which had been my home for the past year or so. My eyes were welled up with tears. As I stood there waiting for the base bus, kids in uniform were walking up the gang plank that I had just walked down, for the last time. The bus came by and I grabbed it to the parking lot and loaded up my car.

THIRTY EIGHT
IN THE REAR VIEW MIRROR

The sky was blue and white puff clouds were passing overhead as I put my bags in the trunk. I kept my hat on the front seat and put the top down. I checked myself in the mirror and noted how sharp I looked in my crisp whites. It was about one o'clock in the afternoon as I headed for the main gate, and I knew I could make it halfway home by midnight. As I passed through the gate for the last time, I was still wondering how the navy missed my being scheduled for Captains Mast. Man, was I lucky. As far as my court date in three weeks for drinking as a minor? Fuck them; I would never be coming back to Florida!

Once I got outside Jacksonville and the traffic thinned out, the sign said New York 950 miles, and I relaxed for the long drive home. I would have plenty of time to reflect on the miracle of what just happened today, as well as the past four years of my life, beginning with the fact that I wasn't going home on leave. This was a one way trip and I wouldn't be coming back. Almost four years had gone by yet it didn't feel that way. It was like I had been on an adventure, away in a foreign place, with things happening all around me that I never experienced before, and yet knew how to handle. So much had happened and I began to realize how lucky I had been. Not just with my recent escapades, but with my life in general. I had just completed a unique life experience and a once in a lifetime journey. I had volunteered to stand behind our President and face whatever may come, in the defense of our country during what could have been the most crucial time in our history. Honestly, I was never more scared then that night we went to General Quarters during the

Cuban Missile crisis back in 1962. I really thought it was all over for me and everyone else in the world.

Thinking back I realized how much different I was now, and how from seventeen to twenty one, the navy had changed me from being a teen with no ambition, into a man. No more negative attitude and 'whoa is me' bullshit. From day one, I learned I had to fit in, get along and be part of a team, or I wouldn't survive. After a short while, I realized I could make friends with people unlike me, or the guys I grew up with and hung around. I learned to respect myself and my shipmates, as well as my service and my country. I learned to live by rules, called the Military Code of Justice. Most of all, I didn't need a club jacket or a candy store as a comfort zone to be a man.

The navy influenced my life in many positive ways, especially in my personal development. I learned to be open-minded and listen. Just as important, I learned control and restraint and how not to panic in a bad situation. They selected me for special skill training as a Radioman, which enabled me to serve on two aircraft carriers allowing me a unique opportunity to cruise the Mediterranean Sea not once, but twice, and see first hand how people lived outside of America. All together, I spent more than a year in the Med with multiple visits to seven European countries. Hell, I even drank vodka with Russian sailors in Istanbul during the cold war.

Onboard the Saratoga and the Roosevelt, I logged over two year's consecutive sea duty. Unfortunately, during that time at sea, I witnessed numerous carrier related accidents resulting in the death of many pilots and seamen. It was heartbreaking to see people killed. For me, it made me better understand and appreciate the sacrifices of military personnel killed in the line of duty, whether in peacetime or war, which can happen maintaining and executing our military might.

For me that part of my life's journey was over now. I had honorably performed my duties as a sailor in the United States Navy. What an experience that had been for me, a kid, who convinced his parents to let him drop out of high school and do what deep inside he knew was necessary for him. Here I was, not even twenty one yet, and I had already seen a good part of the World. How about that?

One thing did make me feel weird. I didn't feel glad that I was getting out. The fact was the Navy never did anything to piss me off. I ended up with this feeling of, okay, you're out now, and you have to go home. But don't worry, if things don't work out, or you get bored, you can always come back. We'll wait for you, but you only have 90 days to let us know. I kind of wished they never talked to me about re-enlisting.

I had a special present for Chas and my mom, something I promised him almost four years ago. I was excited at the thought of giving it to him and seeing his Cheshire grin. It was my General Equivalency High School Diploma.

EPILOG

I made that final drive home with no problem. Thanks Bernie, this was one hell of a car you sold me. Along the way, I picked up an Army guy who rode from Delaware to the Trenton, New Jersey exit on the turnpike. Naturally, I drove straight to my new temporary home at Cal's house. No need to stop home and see the 'baby' in my bedroom.

Cal and I started getting me back into my civilian routine; staying out late and sleeping most of the day. It took me about a week or so before I realized I needed to get a job. Sure enough, Chas hooked me up with the factory he was working so I could be an assembler. It was the same thing over and over for a dollar an hour. Cal lucked out and was hired working on a truck delivering soda. At least he was outside.

I remembered I had this benefit called the GI bill and decided to go to a technical school nearby. I was going at night, after work, and after six months I landed a part time job with McGraw Hill as a computer operator trainee. I started night school in college and after a year and a half, my son was born. I never finished. Five years later, I was a junior executive and moved on to another company and began my climb up the corporate ladder. I never stopped. In 2001, I retired at the age of 57, after selling a wireless company I had helped start.

When I look back, I realize that my accomplishments and successes would not have been possible had it not been for the Navy. Joining when I did, their guidance changed me from that disgruntled teen into a man. They helped build my character and ingrained in me something you don't know at the time, but it is there for you later. Call it your persona, your aura, whatever, I call it honor, respect and anything's possible.

I thank you again for reading my story and hope my experiences provide encouragement to those who may be thinking about serving our country. Personally, I wish all young people would serve their country. They may just benefit more than they could ever imagine.

God bless our Military. Thanks to them we are truly the land of freedom and opportunity.

5903900R0

Made in the USA
Charleston, SC
19 August 2010